OF STIGMATOLOGY

D1525516

VERBAL ARTS :: STUDIES IN POETICS

Lazar Fleishman and Haun Saussy, series editors

OF STIGMATOLOGY

Punctuation as Experience

PETER SZENDY
Translated by Jan Plug

Fordham University Press
NEW YORK 2018

Funding for this book was provided in part by the Helen Tartar Memorial Fund.

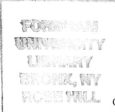

This book was first published in French as *À Coups de points: La Ponctuation comme expérience*, by Peter Szendy © Les Éditions de Minuit, 2013.

Cet ouvrage, publié dans le cadre d'un programme d'aide à la publication, bénéficie de la participation de la Mission Culturelle et Universitaire Française aux Etats-Unis, service de l'Ambassade de France aux EU.

This work, published as part of a program of aid for publication, received support from the Mission Culturelle et Universitaire Française aux Etats-Unis, a department of the French Embassy in the United States.

Olga Ryahovskaya's illustrations of Chekhov's "The Exclamation Mark," appearing in Chapters 1, 5, 6, and 7, are reproduced by courtesy of the artist.

Visit us online at www.fordhampress.com.

Library of Congress Cataloging-in-Publication Data available online at https://catalog.loc.gov.

Printed in the United States of America

20 19 18   5 4 3 2 1

First edition

. . . in the Atom's tomb . . .
—Emily Dickinson

in memoriam Kató Bäck

Contents

Translator's Note

The title of Peter Szendy's book on punctuation, *À Coups de points: La Ponctuation comme expérience*, plays on the idiomatic phrase *coup de poing*, a strike of the fist, a punch. Szendy seemingly pulls that punch, substituting *poing* for the near homophone *points*. No less striking, *À Coups de points* delivers other blows—the points, dots, periods, and other punctuation marks (*point d'exclamation* [exclamation point], *point d'interrogation* [question mark], *deux points* [colon], *point virgule* [semicolon]) that *punchuate* experience with a punctuation that is at once a strike, a blow, a punch. The *point* of Szendy's title reverberates through the many other points in the book, from the *pointillés* of auscultation, to Hegel's *punctum saliens*, to Lacan's *point de capiton*, and beyond. Szendy's text thus formulates a general theory of punctuation in which each of these punctuating points resonates with all the others. If we have chosen to give the book the title *Of Stigmatology*, it is not only because punctuation is also registered in the subtitle, but in order to give the book the proper name of that general theory.

I thank Thomas Szwedska for his meticulous work hunting down references and quotations for this translation. And I owe the author a debt I cannot adequately register—for his careful reading of the translation, for his many suggestions, and for his good-natured responses to my countless questions. Perhaps the best way to begin to repay that debt is by quoting perhaps my favorite of his many messages to me in the attempt to return his wit and unfailing generosity: :-)))) !!!!

Jan Plug

OF STIGMATOLOGY

1 /   Stigmatology

I have never been a big fan of boxing movies, even if I have always admired, for example, Robert De Niro's portrayal of the boxer Jake La Motta in Martin Scorsese's *Raging Bull* (1980). The director has placed the camera in the ring, and we are spared nothing: We see the blows and their immediate repercussions, the spatterings of the beads of sweat, the spurts of blood bursting from the broken arch of the eyebrows. Boxing in general bores me, but I can watch Scorsese's hypnotic images in a continuous loop, images that masterfully make the impact of a fist on a face coincide with the glare of the lights unleashed by the photographers covering the match, who immediately capture and record every gesture. This is especially the case during Jake's final fight, against Sugar Ray Robinson in 1951. The scene is almost unbearable: Jake's face is now nothing but a bleeding fountain from which new showers spurt continuously while countless flashbulbs explode around the ring, light up, take shot after shot from all around the boxer, who can barely stand, decomposing his slow collapse into a discrete series of stroboscopic images.

What, then, fascinates me in these sequences? And why evoke them thus as an epigraph, as if they could put us on the path to what we will be sketching out: a *treatise of general punctuation*?

To be sure, there is the violence of blows filmed so close up that we might believe we are seeing them through a microscope that, paradoxically, sometimes transfigures the cruelty of combat into an almost abstract choreography. Naming this violence here, at the threshold, summoning it at the outset, is a way of stating from the beginning the horizon toward which the pages that follow will tend: the exercise of power that is always inherent in every punctuating gesture. For punctuation is never merely a matter of style or rhetoric in the common sense: It is force; it is power; it is political decision.

But beyond the possible pleasure or disgust felt at the magnified spectacle of repeated blows, there is something, in the instantaneous echo between the punches and their capture by flash photography, that also seems to point toward the very structure of feeling—of seeing, of hearing, of perceiving in general. The matches staged by Scorsese in the film are indeed like a figure for experience. Not only and banally because, as the director put it, "The ring becomes an allegory of whatever you do in life"[1] (you can see it coming: To be alive is to battle; life is a constant struggle). But also and above all because what strikes me, the blows, the shocks, that affect and solicit me, in short, everything that takes place only really happens to me as an aftereffect [après-coup], however immediate, of the flashing.

The sensations, the events, that strike or dot me must be marked, punctuated, for me to have lived them. And this redoubling is the very condition for me—a self [soi], whatever it be [soit]—to be the theater (I don't dare say the ring) of an experience.

Of course, ordinarily we don't even think about this; we aren't conscious of it. The echo of flash photography that accompanies everything that happens to us like its shadow is generally so minute or fleeting that we could rightly compare it to a subliminal image, to an insert between two frames that doesn't last long enough to make itself seen.

Imagine: Every second, every instant, a sort of double comes to insert itself between you and what happens to you, which it redoubles with its punctuation so that it happens to *you*. A bit like in *Fight Club*, the film directed by David Fincher in 1999, in which the narrator (Edward Norton), without noticing, keeps crossing paths with this strange character named Tyler (Brad Pitt), who soon will haunt him until he understands that he is no doubt a projection of himself. If, at first, he doesn't even notice him—nor do we—it is for the good and simple reason that Tyler appears in furtive and intercalated forms, in what theorists of comic strips would call *inter-images*.[2] One thus has to replay the film in slow motion to see clearly Tyler's first ghostly flash appearance while the narrator, suffering from serious trouble sleeping, is making photocopies at the office he works at in a state of fatigue that seems close to hypnosis. The camera is behind the raised cover of the machine, and we hear the voice-over narrate: "With insomnia, nothing's real. Everything's far away. Everything's a copy of a copy of a copy." It's as though the sentence were scanned by the mechanical glimmers of the photocopier. Tyler-the-double also appears suddenly at the same time as the word *copy*—disappearing immediately in a flash—as though he were the exact copy of this passing instant, or rather the replica, the facsimile of the narrator doubling himself in this other who punctuates everything he lives.[3]

Fight Club is perhaps above all a film about sensation in general, as the opening credit sequence, a kind of epigraph to the narrative, explicitly suggests as it tracks the slow ascent, the path, in the narrator's brain, of an affect—fear—through the neurons and their synapses all the way to the secretion of the drops of sweat streaming down his forehead (Tyler has stuck a gun in his mouth). Then, after this gripping opening, which follows the microscopic emergence of feeling, it quickly becomes a matter of the intensity of sensation, that is, the requirement that one be fully present to what one feels—in short, that one *feel oneself feeling*. Thus, while the narrator gives himself—that is, lets or makes Tyler give him— a chemical burn on his right hand, he first attempts to escape the pain by concentrating on certain images rather than others (we literally enter into his imagination to see him push from his mind still images of fires). But his double is there precisely to try to re-center him on the fullness of pure sensation. Tyler slaps the narrator, hits him in the face, telling him, "This is the greatest moment of your life and you're off somewhere missing it": a line that could hold for every instant, every atom, of experience, which not only leaves its marks or stigmata in the flesh **WHAP!** but must also, in order truly to imprint itself, be doubled by the blow that marks it.

Let's not be too quick, then, especially to project onto these scenes from *Fight Club* a clinical or psychologizing diagnosis (of the sort: This guy is sick; he's in the midst of a sadomasochistic delirium, and, on top of that, he's hallucinating; he hears voices). If I evoke these scenes, it is, like the boxing sequences in *Raging Bull*, as allegories of the punctuated structure of experience. Tyler says explicitly to the incredulous narrator, when in the end he is reluctant to recognize the true identity of his double: "People do it every day; they talk to themselves." And he's right: I am constantly addressing myself—including silently—and I am sure that you too, under your breath, with or without words, in the same way hammer out and give rhythm to everything that happens to you.

Perhaps you even go so far as to hit yourself (as in: Pinch me, I'm dreaming; punctuate me so that I feel). Perhaps in the end you look like this narrator fighting an astonishing boxing match with himself throughout the film, a fight that, seen from the outside, seems almost Chaplinesque in its absurdity: At the end, on the surveillance screens of a parking lot, we see a guy in the process of beating himself up. But we know, you and I, that the narrator punches himself above all to try to coincide with what he is living. To nail himself to sensation, to pin himself to what is lived, to try to be the subject who could say: I feel, I am.

And this is what we will have to think, therefore: Punctuation as the doubling blow, as the singular flash or clap that, remarking what happens, allows us to have and to inscribe an experience of it.

It will be argued that, taken so broadly, punctuation no longer has much to do with the manuals that teach us to place the divisions, the breaths, and the scansions of a sentence or speech. But are we so sure of this? It could be, on the contrary, that there is much more than a vague analogy between a comma and a left jab, between quotation marks and a photographic flash. It is their structural affinity that I will attempt to lay out in terms of their *punchuation*.

To such a thinking of punctuation I will give the name *stigmatology*. Why this old, this rare word, that one comes upon only in the dusty pages of ancient volumes more or less forgotten today?[4]

Because we hear in it, on the one hand, the ancient Greek names designating the punctuating mark of the grammarians, equivalents of the Latin *punctum*: *stigma* or *stigmē*, derived from the verb *stizein*. But, on the other hand, because we must listen as well to all the other senses of this verb, which means to sting, to tattoo, to mark with an imprint, and even to cause contusions or to cover with bruises. Thus, like Jake La Motta or the narrator of *Fight Club*, Xanthias, in line 1296 of Aristophanes' *Wasps*, complains of being covered in bruises (*stizomenos*) after having been beaten with a club.

The field of stigmatology thus turns out to be immense. Infinite and heterogeneous, one might say worriedly, since any attempt to map it seems destined to produce an inventory that would take the form of a Borgesian list, like the one that made Michel Foucault laugh in the preface to *The Order of Things*.

Let us try nonetheless to get an overview.

Under the title of stigmatology, we will thus of course study the repertory of punctuation marks in all their arrangements and combinations, including the most complex or contradictory ones, and even in their so-called pure or absolute usages, that is to say, isolated, without either words or phrases that carry them (as when Victor Hugo is said to have asked his editor about the sales of *Les Misérables* by telegraphing him a "?" only to receive a "!" by way of response). Very quickly we will no doubt see that this first area—supposedly that of punctuation in the so-called strict sense of the term—is impossible to circumscribe rigorously: Besides the punctuation of sentences, there is what literary theorists call the punctuation of the page or work. The concept of punctuation thus overflows itself in all directions, since it ends up including blank spaces as well as chapter breaks or the luxuriant outgrowth of an illumination, going so far as to take over, in a poet such as Edward Estlin Cummings, the internal space of a word.[5]

That is why it will be difficult to decide where punctuation properly speaking ends and where its analogic or metaphoric use begins. The great eighteenth-century landscape artist Lancelot "Capability" Brown, like the musicians who—we will return to this—think of melody according to a model of the phrase or phrasing, spoke of the art of gardens in terms of periods and commas. The practice of medical auscultation, which, we will see, Nietzsche generalizes into a paradigm for thinking, is conceived by Laënnec, its inventor, in terms of punctuating or dotted percussion. And Walter Murch, best known as Francis Ford Coppola's editor for films such as *Apocalypse Now* and *The Conversation*, for his part describes the exercise of looking as a rhythmic, phrasing scansion by the blinking of the eye: "We blink to separate and punctuate," he notes, before concluding that "we must render visual reality discontinuous, otherwise perceived reality would resemble an almost incomprehensible string of letters without word separation or punctuation."[6] From page to landscape, from musical bar to the batting of an eyelid, stigmatology will not merely notice and accept as a stopgap this oscillation, this indefinition that affects the concept of punctuation and allows its seemingly limitless extension into such diverse domains. It will be, quite precisely, at once its name and what is at play in it.

Stigmatology will thus be concerned with all kinds of punctuating effects and with all the figures of experience as punctuation. It will describe the "physiognomy" of the different types of marks, like Adorno, who compared the exclamation point to an "index finger raised in warning," the question mark to a "blink of an eye," or the semicolon to a "drooping mustache" whose "gamey taste" he said he enjoyed. It will be interested in all the reappropriations and reinventions of punctuation, in comedians such as Victor Borge or Gad Elmaleh, as well as in the practice of emoticons, in which typographic signs are constantly recombined in a changing repertory:[7] The now classic *smiley* and *frowny*, which put the smile :-) and unhappiness :-(in a binary opposition, have proliferated into a range of affects that go from the state of shock :-o to hysterical laughter :-D passing by way of tears :'(or cruelty >:-) and giving rise to countless variants like the Japanese wink (^, ~) or the indication of deference by kneeling (imagine yourself on all fours, Orz or Or2, your round head followed by your arms and folded legs).

When taken to the point of composing a businessman wearing a tie :-) <///////> or a vampire's pointy incisors ^, . . . ,^ punctuation becomes pictography. As in *Tristram Shandy*, the Laurence Sterne novel that we will deal with at length, it becomes drawing, it crystallizes, it erects and monumentalizes itself into an image.

"A fiery comma flew like a meteor through the cluster of dark, smiling clouds. . . . It was followed by a second and a third, and soon the endless dark background unfolding before his imagination was covered with dense clusters of flying commas."[8]

Thus begins Perekladin's nightmare in Chekhov's brief short story titled "The Exclamation Mark."

On Christmas Eve, after having been the object of criticism and mockery because of the basic level of his education and his empirical use of punctuation marks, Efim Perekladin, collegiate secretary, went to bed feeling wounded. "When you insert a comma, you have to know why" (3), a young man told him, not respecting his forty years of service and experience as a civil servant.

Pondering these vexing remarks while quietly relaxing in bed, Perekladin thus first dreams about commas. Large numbers of them appear, and this irruption gives him a chance at consolation: He tells himself that he is indeed capable of "find[ing] a place for each one of them," that he can place them "consciously," knowingly and without making a mistake (4). Commas then disappear from his dream and are replaced by "fiery periods" (4). Here again, Perekladin congratulates himself on knowing how to use them, so much so that the periods, now mixing with the returning commas, form a "whole host of semicolons and colons" (5), for which the secretary again finds the correct uses. The review, the dream examination, continues successfully as the question marks start to "do the can-can" before "nodd[ing] their hooks approvingly" and "stretch[ing] out into exclamation marks as if under command" (5).

It is here that the real troubles begin, here that the sweet torpor of the dream is transformed into a nightmare that will continue even upon waking. Perekladin, who has never used it in the administrative documents he composes, does not know what to do with this last punctuation mark. Exclamation points wait, they smile—but it's a "hypocritical," even threatening, smile— and all end up melting "into one huge exclamation mark" (6). Perekladin opens his eyes and sits up in his bed. He has a headache, breaks out in a cold sweat. "The exclamation mark no longer stood before his closed eyes, but in front of him, in the room . . . and it was winking slyly at him" (7). The punctuation mark has become embodied in the real; it has become a tangible hallucination.

This delirious vision torments him all night, and even daylight seems unable to make it go away. When he decides to go out, it is actually an exclamation point that has taken the place of the driver of the cab he hails. And when he arrives at his director's house and goes to "sign the guest book because it's a holiday"—the porter is nothing other than an exclamation point, just like the pen case and pen Perekladin takes hold of. It is thus the punctuation mark itself that he picks up and dips in ink in order to sign with it:

"Collegiate Secretary Efim Perekladin!!!"

And as he inserted those three exclamation marks he experienced exultation, indignation, joy and burning rage.

"Take this! Take this!" he muttered, pressing hard with his pen.

The exclamation mark was satisfied and vanished. (7)

So ends the story.

Why have I followed this singular "Christmas tale" through the twists and turns of its details? Why tell it here almost *verbatim* (or rather point by point, *punctatim*)?

Even if it is generally classified under the rubric of comic tales, "The Exclamation Mark" has never made me laugh. I cannot stop myself from taking it very seriously—to the letter even, or to the point [*au point*]. For what is at stake, in this apparently light and fantastical little story, is nothing less than the question of the subject: "I."

Who punctuates whom—or what—in this allegory-like tale? Common sense would suggest that it is of course Perekladin who punctuates sentences, official documents, even his signature. But is this indeed the case?

The impertinent young man who doubts the competence of the respectable civil servant is perhaps not wrong after all, when he says to Perekladin, "Your unconscious . . . spelling, . . . well it's not even worth a kopeck. It's just like being on a mechanical production line" (3). The problem is not, as one might believe from a first, quick reading, knowing whether or not the collegiate secretary is "conscious" of the rules of punctuation, if he punctuates knowingly or "willy-nilly" (4), that is, out of habit. Indeed, if Perekladin's punctuation can be called "unconscious," it is because it operates unbeknown to him, especially when he is dreaming. We cannot consider Perekladin to be punctuating, then, since it is, rather, the marks that decide in him and about him, despite him: The question marks nod their hooks "approvingly"; they turn into exclamation points, just as periods and commas had previously combined into semicolons and colons, without their dreamer having a word to say about it. These are punctuation marks that work together, following their own laws, the poor civil servant having no control or mastery over them; on the contrary, they dictate his actions to him, his sleeping or waking, going so far as to transfigure the real for and in spite of him.

No, Perekladin does not punctuate, then. It is he who is punctuated. And he is perhaps nothing other than an effect of those punctuations that traverse him, constitute him, make him act.[9] That push him, for example, to sign furiously, pressing angrily on the point of his punctuating pen—there!, yes!, take that! —hammering and nailing his name all the more frenetically since he has to reappropriate it in order to say, in the fiction of adhering to himself: "I, Efim Perekladin, I sign!"

In fact, one punchuation is not enough. It takes three to come to the end of the haunting of the exclamation point, to be sure it is "satisfied" and to make it disappear—apparently— in favor of his signature.

Look at them, these three marks planted, riveted one after and on top of the other:

$$! \; ! \; !$$

There is something in this of an abridged formula for the impossibility, for all the Perekladins in the world, for you and me, of coinciding with ourselves, of securing ourselves to ourselves to be able to say "I." For clearly, to be able to sign as that (I) which I am, a mark is not enough. This mark must still be *overpunctuated*; its punctuation must be punctuated, to be sure that the "I" thus stitched and nailed to itself no longer gets carried away in the drift of its hallucinations, that it is really and truly stopped, anchored somewhere.

Hence this aporia, what we might call *Perekladin's paradox*: I cannot say "I" (to myself) except by repeating and multiplying precisely what is to be silenced, that is, those exclamation points that separate me from myself and lead me elsewhere, outside myself despite myself. It is as though I could only sign by punctuating this affirmation of myself with the instrument of the loss of self.

We will also have to think this logic of overpunctuation or punctuating escalation by rereading certain pages from Hegel, Nietzsche, Lacan, and Derrida. Why and how is the point, the figure par excellence of gathering into unity with the self, of bringing together and concentrating into the self, immediately destined to be dispersed and multiplied?

This systolic and diastolic movement, this *discontraction*, is perhaps the very rhythm of punctuation, the punctuating pulsation of punchuations. And it is the beatings of this movement that we are preparing to auscultate.

2 / From the *Rubrica* to the *Smiley*: A Portable History

Facedwiththecountlesstreatisesandarchives—sorry, I forgot the spaces, the blanks. I was going to let myself go writing, as was done in antiquity, in *scriptio continua*.

Faced with the countless treatises and archives handed down by the tradition, I was saying, I feel a bit like the entomologist William Legrand, one of the characters in Poe's "The Gold-Bug," who has to go through many a trial before he can get his hands on what he is looking for. Once one has got it into one's head, as I have, to compile a pocket history of punctuation without being in any way a seasoned philologist, well versed in the difficulties in deciphering Egyptian hieroglyphs or manuscripts from Greco-Roman antiquity, one has every chance of finding oneself perplexed before what will look more or less like this:

53‡‡†305))6*;4826)4‡.)4‡);806*;48†8¶ . . .[1]

In this encoded message, written in red on an old parchment, Legrand laments that there are "no divisions between the words," which would have made the task "comparatively easier" ("Gold-Bug," 262). He nevertheless succeeds in penetrating the secret of the cryptography by calculating the frequency of each of the characters that compose it, which allows him to find its English equivalent. But he then faces another difficulty, since he must now punctuate it in order to read. "My first endeavor was to divide the sentence into the natural division intended by the cryptographist," he explains to the narrator, who asks him: "You mean, to punctuate it?" And Legrand answers: "Something of that kind" (266). The instructions given by the text once it is phrased in this way will lead to the hidden treasure, not without passing through other forms of pointing [*pointage*] or focusing [*mise au point*]: By "pointing the glass" in the right direction Legrand will discover, visible from "no other point of view," a "white spot" that will connect him to the spot where the precious spoils are located (268–69).

I certainly do not have the talent for cryptography or cracking codes that Legrand shows. I will therefore allow myself to be guided by those who are able to decipher sources inaccessible to me, contenting myself with taking notes, like those copyists who, at the beginning of Balzac's *Colonel Chabert*, write what is dictated by a clerk. Who, moreover, does not fail to specify the punctuation: "mark of admiration and six periods," he orders them, so that they write what we would today call an exclamation point, followed by a few more ellipsis points than usual.[2]

The first that I will copy out thus, pointing in passing to this or that of his remarks, is the Belgian Egyptologist Jean Winand, who offers a reconstruction of the history or prehistory of punctuation well before Aristophanes of Byzantium and his disciple Dionysius Thrax, who are traditionally credited with the invention of punctuation in the second century BCE.[3]

What are these arche-punctuations whose traces are going to be lost in the mists of time? And what might they tell us, these ancient punctuating gestures of which we are no doubt the distant heirs without knowing it? Let's try to learn just enough about them to support this statement, which is apparently simple, but whose consequences we will meditate upon endlessly: Punctuation punctuates *after the fact*.

First, there was the *rubrica*, that is, the use of red (*rubricus* in Latin) to distinguish and highlight certain words or signs in relation to others, these written in black ink. Used by the scribes to divide, articulate, and arrange their writings, the practice of the aforementioned *rubrica*—from which the word *rubric* derives—seems to bring together the functions of what we would today call a punctuation of the work and the page, even the sentence:

> In the tales of the New Empire in particular, the rubric is sometimes employed systematically to bring out the narrative structure. The different episodes that make up the story are ordinarily introduced by a stereotypical expression, most often a temporal locution. In carefully prepared manuscripts, this latter is rubricked. Within an episode, the rubric serves again to separate certain narrative conventions. . . . Depending on the case, the rubric corresponds, therefore, *mutatis mutandis*, either to the indication of a new paragraph or, more rarely,

to a strong punctuation. (Winand, "La Ponctuation avant la ponctuation," 166)

Later, the scribes will use points in the strict sense, that is, punctiform
points • that are "regularly evidenced in Egypt beginning in the New Empire, from the eighteenth dynasty on" (169), and which, generally, will
also be written in red, since they play a role analogous to that of the rubric. It seems, however, that in the texts that have come down to us, these
points were never traced "as the scribe wrote": Punctuation by means of
points, Winand writes, was "always done *later*, once the text was totally
written" (170, my rubric or emphasis). And even *much* later, as in the case
of "certain literary manuscripts of the Middle Empire [that] were punctuated, sometimes aberrantly, by New Empire scribes" (170).[4]

The point therefore punctuates retroactively (*nachträglich*, as I will put
it later, with Freud and Lacan). It inscribes the rhythm of a rereading or
reappropriation. In other words, the *punchuation* [coup de point] *is done
after the fact* [après coup], or better, in the gap of its repercussion, however instantaneous or deferred. And if, as Winand suggests, punctuation
by rubricking or points issues from accounting practices,[5] then we find in
the tallying [*pointage*] to verify the lines of an account the paradigm for
the gesture that

✓ reviews

✓ looks through again

✓ retraces

✓ goes back over

the spacing of writings, overpunctuating them with the point of a stylus
or of anything that marks.

At the root of these Egyptian arche-punctuations whose origin gets
lost in the mists of time there is therefore a close solidarity between the
punctuating point and calculation that we should remember when, with
Heidegger and Carl Schmitt, we follow further what the latter called the
punctualism of every thinking of values.

Closer to us, other sequences in the history of punctuation testify to
its post-synchronization, if I dare put it this way. Thus, after *scriptio continua* (withoutseparationbetweenthewords) was adopted in Greece, then
in Rome,[6] it was up to the *grammatici* to teach *praelectio*, a kind of pre-
reading that consisted in annotating the text in order to make it readable—"so that young people can easily and distinctly follow the writings

with their eyes" (*ut facile atque distincte pueri scripta oculis sequintur*), says Quintilian in his *Institutio oratoria* (2.5). Signs of connection or separation (*hyphen* and *diastole*) were introduced, oblique marks that allowed one to identify certain long vowels as well as indications (called *positurae*) of the length of the pauses to be marked. In his *Ars grammatica*, the grammarian Aelius Donatus, who lived in the fourth century BCE and who was Saint Jerome's tutor, recommended three types of pause: the longer one, the *distinctio*, was indicated by a point placed above the line of writing (•), whereas the *media distinctio* and then the *subdistinctio*, the shortest, were noted by points placed in the middle (•) and at the bottom (•) respectively. In *Technē grammatikē*, attributed to Dionysius Thrax (second century BCE), the section on punctuation (*peri stigmēs*) already proposes an analogous repertory, also composed of three points (*teleia*, *mesē*, and *hupostigmē*), the first being the sign (*sēmeion*) of a completed thought (*dianoiās apērtismenēs*). These devices meant to help phrase the text varied, however, and each reader used them differently, as Malcolm Parkes emphasizes in what no doubt remains the best overall study of the history of punctuation in the West:

> Not only are there different systems of punctuation in the surviving *codices distincti* [a *codex* was called *distinctus* when it was emended with punctuation marks] but different readers using the same system indicated pauses in different places in the text, and, where the system permitted, indicated pauses of different length in the same position. Such differences between the punctuation marks, and their use . . . demonstrate the essentially eclectic nature of ancient punctuation: the readers' marks record individual interpretations of the texts.[7]

Parkes also relates that, beginning in the fourth century CE, aristocrats, "amateur scholars," began in a sense to *sign* their punctuations, claiming paternity over them with inscriptions in the manuscript books in their possession. In this way, a certain Flavius Turcius Rufius Apronianus Asterius, who was born into old Roman nobility and held various honorific offices, insisted on writing in his copy of a text by Virgil that he had "read and punctuated" it (*legi et distincxi codicem*) when he was consul in 494. Later, Aurelius Memmius Symmachus, who belonged to one of the most influential families of senators in Rome (the Symmachi), likewise indicated that he had "emended and punctuated" (*emendabam vel distinguebam*) a copy of Macrobius's *Commentary on the Dream of Scipio*.

Stamping or marking with one's imprint the points with which one punctuates, countersigning the stigmatic marks and *distinctiones* with which one spaces the text—we recognize here that logic of overpunctuation whose many other effects we will encounter, for what we see at work in these ancient initialized punctuations, as under Perekladin's pen, is the point that points to itself, that doubles and divides itself by reinscribing itself.

Were one to follow the subsequent history of punctuating practices, from the Middle Ages to our times, one would come across astonishing formulations and metaphors that sometimes have long lives. Like that of Cassiodorus, who in the sixth century tried to systematize the study of punctuation and who in his *Institutiones divinarum et saecularium litterarum* (1.15.12) compares pauses or points (*positurae seu puncta*) to the paths that meanings can take (*quasi quaedam viae sunt sensuum*). Centuries later, Adorno will say nothing else when he speaks of punctuation marks as "traffic signs": "Exclamation points are red," he writes, "colons green, dashes call a halt."[8]

The conventions of these discursive traffic rules change considerably, of course, over their history. Certain traffic signs or signals disappear; others enter the scene. And new ones are called for constantly. Molière's first biographer, Jean-Léonor Le Gallois de Grimarest, did so when he wrote in 1707:

> It would be desirable to allow into our language marks [*Points*] of imperative; of irony; of contempt; of anger; of love & of hate; of joy & of sorrow: reading would be much easier with them.[9]

In the third chapter of his *Traité*, Grimarest defines punctuation as "the art of marking, with small characters, the places in a discourse where one must pause and the meaning one must give to expression" (46–47). He then enters into an inventory of the punctuation marks in use in his time:

> the closing Mark (.) the Mark of admiration (!) the questioning Mark (?) & the interrupting Mark (. . .) the colon : the semi-colon ; & the Comma. (47)[10]

A strange list in which, read from today's point of view, we cannot really distinguish examples or *mentions* of punctuation from their *use*. Especially when the author suddenly drops from the enumeration those parentheses that nevertheless make it readable. (Reread, you'll see.)

When Grimarest demands more marks than are available, then, he not only heralds a certain page from Rousseau, who, fifty years later, in his *Essay on the Origin of Languages*, will regret the absence of a "vocative mark" in French.[11] He also anticipates the more fantastical dreams of authors closer to us: In *L'Ostensoir des ironies* (1899), Alcanter de Brahm —an anagram of Marcel Bernhardt—claimed he had invented the irony mark (which resembles the inverted Spanish question mark: ¿), and Hervé Bazin, in *Plumons l'oiseau*, in 1966 called for six additional "intonation marks" (of irony, doubt, certitude, acclamation, love, and authority). To which we should of course add today the countless *smileys* or emoticons whose use has become the rule and whose history is beginning to be written.[12]

In addition to their number, the place of punctuation marks also varies. Grimarest—him again—in his *Traité* wished that "the admiration and question mark preceded the sentence, rather than closing it, because one needs a great deal of practice reading to pick up on the tone that suits these two figures without guidance" (53–54). But in the absence of such a punctuating practice—¡it would resemble that of today's Spanish!— Grimarest resigns himself to the following recommendation:

> Since we are not ordinarily prepared, when we read, I would not recommend undertaking it to anyone who is not in the habit of foreseeing the movements from the first terms that express them: for a passion, a figure poorly executed, is no pleasure to the auditor. (99)

Grimarest's worry over exclamation and question marks must be taken very seriously. It should probably be understood even beyond its apparent object, the adequation and stability of intonation when reading aloud. For one could of course have the same fears not only regarding the place of all the emoticons in the world—should one place them before or after the statement they are supposed to modalize, for example ironizing or attenuating it?—but also regarding the correct position of the apparently most banal, phlegmatic, and impassive marks, such as the period, the comma, and the semicolon. Indeed, how to detect in the course of speech (whether addressed to oneself or others) if the next intersection will be a stop or a yield, a roundabout or an entrance onto the highway—I am extending, as you will have understood, Cassiodorus's metaphor, which Adorno updated. How to know this when it is at the end of the journey, at the end of the sentence, that one encounters the highly anticipated signage?

"One must . . . guess it," says Grimarest, who notes that "the most skillful readers have great difficulty, on first reading, getting the meaning of a work" (54). Put differently: Punctuation marks are anticipated; one gets out ahead of them; one sees them coming; and from the end of the sentence toward which the reader is already headed, they in a sense redound in advance or have immediate repercussions on what is nevertheless still to be read, said. Such is the elasticity of marks that I will try to think in all of its generality with Hegel when he borrows from physiology the notion of *punctum saliens*. That is, literally, of the leaping or jumping point.

But first, it is time for us to look at punctuation at work, in the most gripping and inventive manner possible, in a novel, Sterne's *Tristram Shandy*, published in nine volumes, between 1759 and 1767. I can scarcely think of an equivalent: This singular autobiography is also, as we will see, a staging of points that remains unparalleled in the history of literature.

3 / The Point of (No) Monument, or Tristram's Cut

We were expected there, anticipated.

As if on the lookout for the one who is going to read it, the text worked in advance to give rhythm to, that is, to punctuate (for) its reader.

But such is the case, you will tell me, of every self-respecting text. Of course. Except that *Tristram Shandy* does not merely prescribe the phrasing of each of the sentences that compose it; what the novel also seems to capture is the movement, the tempo, of reading in general, whatever it reads. In fact, when the narrator writes,

... and so read

on — — — — — — — —

— — — — — — — — —

— — — — — — — — —

— — — — — — — — —

— — — — — — — — —,[1]

he inscribes, as it were, the beat, the rhythm, of reading as such.

Our place as readers is thus already marked multiply in *Tristram Shandy*, even before we approach it. But for me, this place was no doubt over-determined, it was overpointed [*surpointée*], as it were, for the name of the protagonist, the name Shandy, had in advance taken on a curious resonance in my ears. Yes, *Shandy*: To my amusement or embarrassment, depending on the context and the mood, that is one of the distorted pronunciations of my name that has marked—punctuated—so many decisive moments in my life, from elementary school to university and beyond. Sometimes surprised, sometimes irritated—how many times have I heard myself called *Shandy*, Peter *Shandy*?

To be sure, there were more serious and consequential distortions, such as the one that made my name absolutely unrecognizable at the very instant my lot in military service was decided (I remained alone, the last person in a squalid parade ground, not having understood that I had been called by the name Seznoy). There have been lighter and more amusing distortions too, like the ticket from a Chinese dry cleaner in New York on which I was inscribed as Sgengy. But it is undoubtedly *Shandy* that will have been my most common *shibboleth*, the sign of the banality of my foreignness, which allowed me to understand how difficult it was to get my name across the border from my father's Hungary to the France that took him in in 1956.

I have to admit, then, that in a sense I had adopted Sterne's novel even before having read it, because of its title, which already intrigued me and in which I saw something like the promise of a borrowed autobiography, signed by another, but with my distorted name. And that is why, reading it for the first time, I imagined, in any case, that *I would find myself in it*, without knowing yet that what awaited me were rather the meanderings, the countless detours, of the attempt at narrating that, several times, allows the inexorable formula of its failure to be heard:

> Write as I will, and rush as I may into the middle of things . . .—I
> shall never overtake myself—whipp'd and driven to the last pinch,
> at the worst I shall have one day the start of my pen—and one day is
> enough for two volumes—and two volumes will be enough for one
> year. (228–29)

This lag between life and its writing, this gap can only be stopped by death, which alone could make possible—and, by the same fatal blow, impossible—a strictly autobiographical writing.[2] Between the gallop or race [*la course*] of the signifier and the course [*le cours*] of life, there is a sliding, a perpetual disconnect, that nothing, no anchoring, will be able to fill in or reduce to a self-coincidence of which the narrator would be the subject.

I would like to put forward the hypothesis—we will verify it—that this is why Sterne uses punctuation in a way that remains unparalleled in literature, before and after him. Many commentators have in fact highlighted this: He multiplies and remultiplies marks [*points*] of all sorts (points properly speaking, but also dashes of varying lengths, asterisks, blank

or black pages . . .), as though most at stake for him were

stopping, interruption, and even—we will come to this—the interruption of interruption, in an infinite and infinitely staged search for what might finally fasten the text to its pinned down subject. The punctuation of *Tristram Shandy* thus reveals an incessant pursuit of what we might name anchoring, or better, the *button point* [*point de capiton*] of autobiography.[3]

Yes, the subject of autobiographical discourse should already be pinned to itself, so that its "monument," as Rousseau said of his *Confessions*, his "only certain monument," can be erected.[4] And this monumental erection of the self would be made possible by the pricking or puncture that would secure the subject to itself. That is, as we will read explicitly in Sterne's novel, by the symbolic law of a *cut* that, stopping the movement in the course of which the "I" endlessly escapes itself, would make it finally coincide with itself in the text.

What in fact happens in the sixteenth chapter of the fifth volume? We witness there the writing of a book—a book in the book, then. And as it is written it is irremediably distanced by its object, none other than Tristram himself. Just as Tristram can declare that he will never catch up with himself in his narrative of himself ("I shall never overtake myself"), so too the gap between writing and life here impedes the completion of the *Tristrapaedia*, this treatise undertaken by the narrator's father about, and for the education of, his son: The "slow progress" in his writing means that, after "three years and something more, indefatigably at work," father Shandy has "scarce completed, by his own reckoning, one half of his undertaking" (300). But this delay is doubled again; it soon becomes abyssal, since the offspring whose growth the *Tristrapaedia* attempts to capture constantly escapes description:

> The misfortune was, that I was all that time totally neglected and abandoned to my mother; and what was almost as bad, by the very delay, the first part of the work, upon which my father had spent the most of his pains, was rendered entirely useless,——every day a page or two became of no consequence.——
>
> . . .
>
> In short, my father . . . advanced so very slow with his work, and I began to live and get forwards at such a rate, that if an event had not happened——which, when we get to it, if it can be told with decency, shall not be concealed a moment from the reader——I verily believe, I had put by my father . . . to be buried under ground. (300–1)

The son's escape from the father's educational discourse can be stopped, it seems then, by the event in question, which, as the seventeenth chapter relates, is none other than an accidental circumcision, verging upon castration. The chambermaid, having forgotten to place a pot under the bed of little Tristram, then five years old, suggests that he relieve himself otherwise: "lifting up the sash with one hand . . . and helping me up into the window seat with the other" (301). But then "slap came the sash down like lightening upon us" (301), followed by the chambermaid's cries, which, punctuated as they are by long dashes, imply at first that the child has been completely emasculated: "Nothing is left,—cried *Susannah*,—nothing is left—for me, but to run my country.——" (301).

Here more than ever, punctuation by dashes, points of a sort, stretched out into an inchoative line, is at once an interruption of the flow of writing or reading and a call to follow. Like an obstacle course, the punctuation remarks, repeats, and reinscribes in the phrasing the cut of Tristram's (quasi) castration, while also letting it float suspended in the course of the text that is always to come: By stretching the sentence like an elastic strained to the point of breaking, each dash is *on the point* of cutting it as it retraces with its mark the very continuity of the statement.

Yet we have read that the event of this cut, Tristram himself said, was supposed to stop the son's escape by attaching him to his father's *Tristrapaedia* ("he advanced so very slow with his work, and I began to live and get forwards at such a rate, that if an event had not happened,—which, when we get to it, if it can be told with decency, shall not be concealed a moment from the reader . . .").

Is this indeed the case?

When the father later learns of the accident (in the twenty-sixth chapter), he declares, "I thought as much" (307). As though, as the author of the Tristrapaedic treatise, but also as the author of its living subject (his son), he could or should have anticipated the episode:

> One would imagine from this——. . . that my father before that time, had actually wrote that remarkable chapter in the *Tristrapaedia*, which to me is the most original and entertaining one in the whole book; —and this is the *chapter upon sash-windows* . . .—I have but two reasons for thinking otherwise.
>
> First, Had the matter been taken into consideration, before the event happened, my father certainly would have nailed up the sash-window for good an' all;—which, considering with what difficulty he composed books,—he might have done with ten times less trouble, than he could have wrote the chapter: this argument I foresee holds good against his writing the chapter, even after the event; but 'tis obviated under the second reason, which I have the honour to offer to the world in support of my opinion, that my father did not write the chapter upon sash-windows and chamber-pots, at the time supposed,—and it is this.
>
> ——That, in order to render the *Tristrapaedia* complete, —I wrote the chapter myself. (307)

The son will therefore have completed the *Tristrapaedia* to which he ought to have been fastened by the button point of his castration. The father's incomplete treatise thus becomes a simple part of the general tristramography, of this impossible autobiography titled *The Life and Opinions of Tristram Shandy, Gentleman*, in which the narrator constantly restarts his race after himself. A race after his self-coincidence that is also, as we have already glimpsed and as several passages in the seventh volume state explicitly, a *race against death*.[5]

The event of the cut therefore does not have the expected punctuating effect. No more than the son does the father succeed in circumscribing or circumcising the subject of the monumental tristrencyclopedia.

Far from being able to anchor anything or anyone somewhere, the button point is *unbuttoned*.[6]

4 / (Un)Pointings

Why is autobiography—which could be a phallic monument to the sovereignty of the narrator subject securing and fastening himself to himself—condemned to remain aphallous and acephalous, with neither head nor tail?

It is not enough to say allusively, as I just have, that the button point[1] that should stabilize bio-graphic anchoring (the fastening of writing to life) is unbuttoned. We must look still closer, at how in *Tristram Shandy* punctuation and the monumental phallic erection support and refer to one another even as they are caught up in a general movement of dissociation, that is, of unhooking the text and its subject—which precisely no longer belongs to it through and through.

Let us begin again, then, with this question: What is a point[2] from the perspective of a broadened theory of punctuation, in the horizon of a general stigmatology that a book like *Tristram Shandy* calls for on every page?

In addition to the usual punctuation marks in Sterne's time, one must count other typographic devices as points in the broad sense. Sterne's use of common marks already very often takes them in a new direction, as when he lengthens and multiplies dashes to mimic, for example, the slowed-down, jerky pulse of poor Lieutenant Le Fever, who is on the point of death:[3]

> Nature instantly ebb'd again,——the film returned to its place,——
> the pulse fluttered——stopp'd——went on——throbb'd——stopp'd
> again——moved——stopp'd——shall I go on?——No. (343)

The sentence here matches the heartbeat as it nears exhaustion; it reproduces its hesitating palpitation (the *punctum saliens*, as I will put it soon with Hegel), to the point that writing seems literally to cling to life: When the narrator wonders whether he should pursue this phrasing by fits and starts, his response in the negative, the decisive *no* with which he cuts off the beat of the sentence, comes down like a guillotine that at the same time also signs the dying person's *death sentence*.

It is tempting to describe such punctuation as hyperrealist. It could also be called iconic, for example when Sterne doubles deictics and other textual pointers with the icon of an index finger ("☞ This is to serve . . . instead of a whole volume" [91]; "☞This I recommend . . ." [97]; "☞ mark only" [160]). Or again when, in the fourth chapter of the first volume, Tristram advises his hurried reader to

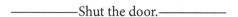

suggesting that he "skip over" the detailed story of his conception, whose threshold is marked by the line crossing the page (8).

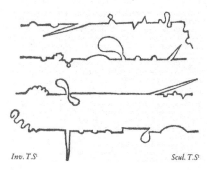

We find this iconicity of punctuation again on the level of metanarrative when the narrator explains and illustrates how he narrates with curves that trace the rhythm of his narrative and its digressions, so many deviations compared to what he falsely presents as the ideal "right line," the "straight" line: "The shortest line, says *Archimedes*, which can be drawn from one given point to another.——" (380).

But with these narratological curves or straight lines it is a question of a punctuation on a larger scale: no longer the punctuation of the sentence but of the plot, although the two can merge, as they do with the interruption that stops the discourse into which Tristram's father was preparing to enter:

as he opened his mouth to begin the next sentence,

Chapter XV

In popp'd Corporal *Trim* . . . (95)

That a chapter break can be equivalent at times to a comma or a dash, at times to a stronger mark, a final period, at times to a veritable gulf in which a whole section of the story is swallowed up, in short, that the punctuation of the work, as it is now called, is open to every possibility is what Tristram himself theorizes several times in what he calls a "chapter upon chapters" (225) or with respect to the "chasm of ten pages" that leaves "a whole chapter wanting here" (251).[4] There seems to be no limit to this poetics of punctuating interruption, which can even cut up the final syllable of a word in order to trace in it a geographic border, as when Corporal Trim tries to tell the "Story of the king of Bohemia and his seven castles":

There was a certain king of Bo--he——
    As the corporal was entering the confines of Bohemia, my uncle Toby obliged him to halt for a single moment. (451)

The repeated interruption of the corporal's narrative, as of so many others, repeats *en abyme* the interruptions that everywhere affect the tristramography, that give it its idiomatic rhythm, its "unique genre" ("a species by itself" [58]), of which the narrator is so proud.[5] At least five times the poor corporal takes up his fable's *incipit* ("There was a certain king of Bohemia") without ever being able to complete it, prevented as he is by Uncle Toby's interventions. Both, furthermore, will end up stating, after various other twists and turns, "What became of that story, Trim?—We lost it, an' please your honour, somehow betwixt us" (468). The will was there, however, since Uncle Toby, for example, "discontinued his dissertation upon gunpowder," *interrupted his own interruption*, and then begged the corporal to "go on" (456). But the interrupted interruption is interrupted in turn, and so on, in the claudicant approach Tristram claims for his narration.

Now, what does it mean, for punctuation, for all kinds of points, to interrupt interruption itself in this way, repeatedly staging what one might call a *general interinterruption*?

This is what we still have to understand, by turning toward the most monumental punctuations that await us in the tristencyclopedia: that of blank, black, or marbled pages.

There are indeed blanks, sorts of holes, in *Tristram Shandy* that the reader is called upon to fill in. A "vacancy," as English puts it literally, to be filled with words, as when the narrator curses his bad idea of selling his chaise, in which he forgot his manuscript notes:

It then presently occurr'd to me, that I had left my remarks in the pocket of the chaise—and that in selling my chaise, I had sold my remarks along with it, to the chaise-vamper.   I leave this void space that the reader may swear into it, any oath that he is most accustomed to——For my own part, if ever I swore a *whole* oath into a vacancy in my life, I think it was into that——. (424–25)

Encouraged to put a swear word in this empty space, the reader also stumbles upon much bigger lacunae that are left open for us to fantasize about, as when an entire page is left blank and each of us is invited to "paint . . . to your own mind" (376).[6]

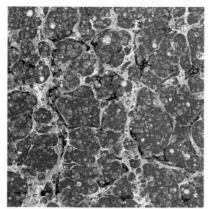

These voids, these gaps in the text, find their response elsewhere, in surpluses, overabundances that make the text, on the contrary, impenetrable, unreadable. A lack or excess in the text, then: These are the two extremes between which tristramographic punctuation oscillates.[7] And in both cases, reading stops *and* restarts there: It is impeded, by excess or lack, finding in this very impediment the most powerful of its resources.

On the side of excess, for example, there is the famous double marbled page that is preceded by this address to the reader:

Read, read, read, read, my unlearned reader! read,—or by the knowledge of the great saint *Paraleipomenon*—I tell you before-hand, you had better throw down the book at once; for without *much reading*, by which your reverence knows, I mean *much knowledge*, you will no more be able to penetrate the moral of the next marbled page (motly emblem of my work!) than the world with all its sagacity has been able to unravel the many opinions, transactions and truths which still lie mystically hid under the dark veil of the blank one. (180)

If the marbled page is thus the emblem of the tristramian work in that its medley of colors and jasperings suggests infinite reading possibilities,  this emblem, as Tristram suggests, seems to draw its emblematic value from reference to an earlier page, another double page, this time black and mysteriously hiding under its veil of ink so many things that are still to be deciphered.

Marble is no doubt the material par excellence of all monuments. And the marbled pages of a book are those that, framing it at its beginning and end, monumentalize texts—in editions that are sometimes called, precisely, monumental. But the most monumental of all the punctuations in *Tristram Shandy*, that punctuation that seems meant to state, sustain, or anchor the truth of all the others, is therefore the double black page that comes to punctuate the death of Pastor Yorick at the end of the twelfth chapter of the first volume.

This page is a funerary monument where we see a point, inflated or  amplified in its blackness, to the point of overflowing the dimensions of the page that contains it: a point becoming a veritable stela, a gravestone that, in addition to the mourning of the character, here inscribes and commemorates the mortuary character of all punctuation, its absolute value as *full stop* [*point final*].

It so happens that, barely a few lines before this monumental black point, anticipating it, we encounter the first, the very first, occurrence of the word *monument* in the novel: "Monumental inscription," writes Tristram (27). Now, this word will recur but once; it will make but one other appearance in the entirety of the nine volumes that make up the tristrencyclopedia. And this second occurrence—no less striking than the first, if we listen to it—takes place in the middle of a discourse by father Shandy on the occasion of the death of one of his sons (Tristram's brother, then). There it is a question of punctuation and monumentality, of those monuments that punctuate death (that are the full stop [*point final*] of death), at the same time that they themselves are deprived of their apex [*pointe*], that is, are *interinterrupted*, punctuated in their very punctuation:

—*To die*, is the great debt and tribute due unto nature: tombs and monuments, which should perpetuate our memories, pay it themselves; and the proudest pyramid of them all, which wealth and science have erected, has lost its apex, and stands obtruncated in the traveller's horizon. (283)

Father Shandy speaks here of the erection of a sort of *monument of monuments*: Contrary to what Charles Mauron's French translation suggests, Sterne in fact mentions, in the singular, "the proudest pyramid of them all," the pyramid or monument par excellence.[8] As though imagining the biggest full stop [*point final*] that could ever have existed, a punctuation so monumental that, to represent it iconically in a book, its blackness would have to fill an entire page.

Now, this monument to monumentality itself, we come to see, is clipped, beheaded, decapitated, or unbuttoned, as if, in order to play its part as the ultimate full stop among all the funerary punctuations, it had to detach itself from itself in order to punctuate itself: to be *its own monument* (one possible definition of autobiography), which is also to say, its own ruin.

 More rigorously still, it must be said that in *Tristram Shandy* the biggest full stop there is, this point of points, is a *double* black page whose status is thus also affected by an irremediable duplicity: Is this point so immense, so monumental, that a single page cannot contain it? Or is it *doubled* in order to punctuate itself, even if this means becoming what Grimarest called the "interrupting mark" (that is, in modern French, ellipses [*points de suspension*])?

The alternative is strictly undecidable, for reasons we have seen. Thus, the *monumental inscription* of Yorick's stela is what we might call, in order to render both senses of the word *point*, the *point of (no) monument*:[9] Its value as substantive (the point as anchoring point, button point, Archimedes' point, or full stop [*point final*]), and its adverbial value as negation (there is no [*point de*] subject, no [*point de*] stability or firm base authorizing the erection of a phallic monumentality). Each mark, in the general theory of punctuation that *Tristram Shandy* calls for, each mark—whether semicolon or dash; whether blank, black, or marbled page; whether indented line or new chapter heading . . . —, each mark is the space of the potential erection of a funerary monument, of a stela for everything that precedes it, safeguarding the stability of a meaning that is thus posited and deposited in it, entrusted to it; but each mark also and at the same time awaits overpunctuation, its monumental phallic power to puncture suspended.

In short, the final full stop, the grandest of all the monuments, remains *divisible*, exposed to its overpunctuation to come, which it already contains and comprehends, which from the start already begins to *(un)point* it.[10]

Is this why Tristram Shandy and *Tristram Shandy* never get *to the point*, as one says in English?

5 /   P.S.: On Restitching
(Lacan vs. Derrida)

Yes, P.S., in order to graft a *post scriptum* to the preceding chapter (and not to inscribe between the lines the initials of some improbable Peter Shandy I might have dreamed up). An appendix, then, to point out the *divisibility* of the point that *Tristram Shandy* stages as a tragicomedy. And which was also, if one knows how to understand it, the crucial stake in the critique Derrida aimed at Lacan,[1] which opened a debate in which age-old questions of the definition of the point are revived in an unprecedented manner.

To situate the import of this debate—it is in no way limited to a point of theory, as we have seen in traversing Sterne's masterful stigmatological narrative—we ought first of all to recall the importance of punctuation in not only Lacan's thought but his practice. For it is first of all the analyst who punctuates:

> This is how he proceeds in the best of cases: he takes the description of an everyday event as a fable addressed as a word to the wise, a long prosopopoeia as a direct interjection, and, contrariwise, a simple slip of the tongue as a highly complex statement and even the rest of the silence as the whole lyrical development it stands in for.
>
> It is therefore a propitious punctuation that gives meaning to the subject's discourse. This is why the ending of the session—which current technique makes into an interruption that is determined purely by the clock and, as such, takes no account of the thread of the subject's discourse—plays the part of a scansion which has the full value

of an intervention by the analyst that is designed to precipitate concluding moments.[2]

Analytic practice, this felicitous punctuation :-) thus takes on a scriptural character, the analyst himself becoming a "scribe" who "punctuates" the "record" of the subject's discourse (258). And the punctuating effect of analytic listening is thus always a way of arresting a meaning:

> It is a fact, which can be plainly seen in the study of symbolic writings, whether the Bible or Chinese canonical texts, that the absence of punctuation in them is a source of ambiguity. Punctuation, once inserted, establishes the meaning; changing the punctuation renews or upsets it; and incorrect punctuation distorts it. (258)

Punctuation is therefore one of the essential resources of the analytic cure. But it is also the pivot in the theory of language that grounds its possibility, since the "button point"—that "punctuation in which signification is constituted"—is thought according to the model of the punctuated sentence:[3]

> The diachronic function of this button point can be found in a sentence, insofar as a sentence closes its signification only with its last term, each term being anticipated in the construction constituted by the other terms and, inversely, sealing their meaning by its retroactive effect. (682)

Now, whether it is a matter of the rhythm of a cure or the conception of signification upon which this cure relies, in the end it is of course the subject that is at stake. A subject that one can thus think, in the image of Perekladin, as at once punctuated and punctuating, as constituted or woven from the effects of punctuation that it punctuates and that punctuate it.[4]

But the point, in Lacan, the concept of the point, is also at work even where it does not appear by name. It is in a sense disguised, hidden beneath an assumed name—the "letter"—smuggling into the theory of language its oldest attributes: its indivisibility, its atomic nature (*atomos* in Greek means that which cannot be cut), and its always localized, situated, character, what one might call its positionality.

The point, at least since the first definition in Euclid's *Elements*, is in fact an atom in space: Called *sēmeion*, as though it were a sign, a sort of indivisible letter, already to speak like Lacan, it has no parts (*sēmeion estin, hou meros outhen*). But already in Aristotle's *Metaphysics*, the point, which is there called *stigmē*, while it is placed or posited somewhere, admits of no partition:

> That which is indivisible in quantity and *qua* quantity is called a . . . point if it is not divisible in any dimension and has position [*thesin ekhon*], a line [*grammē*] if it is divisible in one dimension, a plan if in two, a body if divisible in quantity in all—i.e. in three—dimensions.[5]

Ever since its ancient definitions, the point is thus that which is indivisibly localized somewhere. And as if in a distant, distorted echo of Aristotle, this is also the case of what Lacan calls the letter, that is, the "materiality of the signifier,"[6] which, he writes, is "*singular* in many ways [*bien des points*], of which the first is not [*ne point*] to allow of partition" (16; we can hear one *point* playing against the other here, the adverb against the noun). The letter cannot be cut, therefore ("cut a letter into little pieces, it remains the letter that it is"), and while it is never in its place, while it is constantly changing places and missing from its place, for this very reason it testifies to what Nancy and Lacoue-Labarthe have very good reason to call "the signifier's ability to be located" (28).

Now, these are precisely the two traits or characteristics of the letter— its localization and its indivisibility, inherited from the age-old figure of the point—that Derrida questions at the same time in his critical reading of Lacan, under the title of what he calls the "atomystic," that is, the atomist, punctualist, or stigmatic mystic on which the Lacanian theory of the letter is grounded.[7] For as Derrida shows, the indivisibility of the letter (of the *sēmeion*, of the point or material, signifying atom) is in fact its *ideality*, rooted in the supposed materiality that Lacan claims for it:

> If it [the signifier] were divisible, it could always be lost en route. To protect against this possible loss the statement about the "materiality of the signifier," that is, about the signifier's indivisible singularity, is constructed. *This "materiality," deduced from an indivisibility found nowhere, in fact corresponds to an idealization.* Only the ideality of a letter resists destructive division. . . . This alone permits the singularity of the letter to be maintained [*se garder*]. If this ideality is not the content of meaning, it must be either a certain ideality of the signifier (what is identifiable in its form to the extent that it can be distinguished from its empirical events and re-editions), or the "*point de capiton*" which staples the signifier to the signified. The latter hypothesis conforms more closely to the system. . . . [Lacan] considers the letter only at the point at which it is determined (no matter what he

says) by its content of meaning, by the ideality of the message that it "vehiculates," by the speech whose meaning remains out of the reach of partition, so that it can circulate, intact, from its place of detachment to a place of reattachment, that is, to the same place. In fact, this letter does not only escape partition, it escapes movement, it does not change its place. (464)[8]

The Lacanian letter is therefore the letter that it is—indivisible and singular, atomic—only because it is fastened to a meaning by the punctuation of the button point, to which we thus return. It is as though the debate between Derrida and Lacan on the atomystic came down to the holding point, the point form of buttoning. And it is there, precisely, that we must look closer.

Let's pause for a moment over these pages of the seminar in which Lacan, in the course of a reading of the first scene of Racine's *Athalie*, tries to define, identify, and *localize* a button point: "that point," he says, "around which all concrete analysis of discourse must operate."[9]

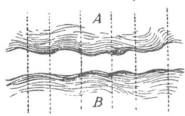

At the beginning of the session of 6 June 1956, Lacan borrows from Ferdinand de Saussure's *Course in General Linguistics* what he calls the "famous schema of the two curves," which he interprets in these terms: "At the upper level Saussure locates the series of what he calls thoughts . . . whereas underneath is the signifier as a pure chain of discourse, a succession of words" (261). Yet toward the end of the same session, it is as if Lacan had implicitly reinterpreted the Saussurean schema in terms of the image of the cross-section of a mattress, a substitution that unleashes and governs the metaphor of quilting [*capitonnage*].[10] Borrowed from the vocabulary of upholstering, the metaphor is then extended very literally when he indicates, points out, in Racine's text the spot where this button point sinks in: "The upholsterer's needle," Lacan writes, has "entered" at the moment in the play when the high priest Joad pronounces the line, "God found faithful in all his threats" (268); and when it "reappears," Lacan continues, "it's all over"—that's the end of it, it's sown up [*ça capitonne*]: Officer Abner declares that he is going to "join the faithful troops" (268).

Lacan therefore describes the movement of a needle that *enters and exits*: the button point, like all sewing [*points de couture*], thus seems to involve a multiplicity of stitches—at least two—in order to "[knot] the signified to the signifier" (268). But, a few lines later, the button point is identified with a word; it is localized in a single substantive:

> The button point is the word *fear*. . . . Everything radiates out from and is organized around this signifier, similar to these little lines of force that an upholstery button forms on the surface of material. It's the point of convergence that enables everything that happens in this discourse to be situated retroactively and prospectively. (268; translation slightly modified—Trans.)

The successive stitches therefore seem to be brought together in a single, unique point, which constitutes the center. It is thus a sort of button that one sees, where the overlapping pieces of cloth are attached, radiating pleats (*button tie*, moreover, is how certain American translators and commentators of Lacan propose to translate this *point de capiton*).[11] What does not appear from that point on, as if the buttoning ultimately masked it, is the inflection, the rhythmic beat or *pulse* of the punctuation that stitches *in double time*, in a sort of echo of itself.

Nevertheless, when Lacan resumes and revives, when, two years later in his seminar,[12] he puts back in play and onstage, this same concept of the button point, he re-elaborates it by restoring to it its temporal pulsation, so to speak, which is that of repercussion or punctuation *after the fact*—in a retroaction, then, which in Freud's German is called *Nachträglichkeit*.

> [A] discourse is not a punctiform event. A discourse is not merely a matter, a texture; it takes time, it has a temporal dimension, a thickness. . . . For example, if I start a sentence, you will not understand its meaning until I have finished it. It is utterly necessary—this is the definition of the sentence—for me to have said the final word for you to understand where the first one is. This gives us the most tangible example of what we can call the *nachträglich* action of the signifier. (15)

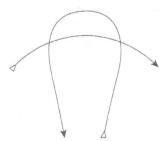

The button point thus takes on a new figure. Again, we find in it the double stitch of the aftereffect [*après-coup*] that had disappeared in the unifying gathering of the buttoning. But this *restitching*, this doubling that makes punctuation a *repunctuation*, appears or reappears only at the cost of a new disappearance, since the schema borrowed from Saussure has now been flattened, crushed in a sense, onto a single plane:

> Let me point out that what these two lines previously represented, that is, the signifier and the signified, cannot be confused with what they represent here, which is slightly different, for now we are placed entirely on the plane of the signifier. The effects on the signified are elsewhere; they are not represented. (15)

The Lacanian reading of Saussure's schema in terms of upholstery is itself reread here in order to be taken in a different direction, into a development that we will not follow (it will end up, after a long and complex elaboration, in what Lacan will later name the "graphs of desire").[13]

What has taken place, then? What has happened to the buttoning point, to its atomic punctiformity?

Lacanian buttoning seems to oscillate, like a sort of heartbeat, between diastolic and systolic movements: between moments of the distension or doubling of the point and moments of stigmatic contraction. Sometimes, for example when it buttons together the plane of the signifier and the plane of the signified, the punctuation of the button point plays a role comparable to that of the *hyphen*, that old prosodic mark that served, like our *trait d'union*,[14] to gather syllables into the unity of a single word (from the Greek *hupo*, "under," and *hen* "one"). Sometimes, on the contrary, when it pricks and repricks in the doubling of its stitch, the upholsterer's needle matches the rhythmic beat of the echo after the fact: It is as though the point were split then; punctuation is more a repercussion that detaches and marks, like the *diastole*, that other old prosodic sign that, contrary to the *hyphen*, separated two syllables liable to get mixed up in a single word.[15]

The atomystic is therefore but one of the tendencies, one of the poles of attraction, in Lacan's signifying stigmatology. For the beat that gives life to this stigmatology also swings, on the other side, toward bursting the punctiformity of the point: As signifiers pass by on the rails of discourse, then, punctuation hits and strikes twice rather than once.

6 / Phrasing, or The Holes in Meaning

Lacan somewhere has this striking, incisive formulation: "A punctuation without a text," he says.[1]

The phrase is found in a passage of the *Écrits* that deals with foreclosure or excision (what Freud called *Verwerfung*), that is, expulsion from the symbolic field. More precisely, Lacan takes the example of Freud's case of the Wolf Man, who in different forms constantly hallucinates about the castration he has radically excluded from all possible symbolization (it is not even the object of repression). Sergei Pankejeff—the real name of the *Wolfsmann*, a Russian aristocrat—has this hallucinatory vision in particular: While making notches in the bark of a walnut tree, he sees himself sever his little finger, which is now attached only by the skin. In other words, as Lacan writes, "Castration—which is excised by the subject here from the very limits of what is possible, but which is also  thereby withdrawn from the possibilities of speech—appears in the real, erratically . . . *like a punctuation without a text*" (324, my emphasis).

What happens with the Wolf Man calls to mind, mutatis mutandis, the hallucinations of another Russian, his name Perekladin: The exclamation points the collegiate secretary does not manage to find a place

for among the written symbols he wields come to haunt him in the real in the form of delirious visions. Luckier than Panke-jeff (who, after his analysis with Freud, still thinks his nose is full of holes, for example), Perekladin, we recall, will be relieved of his torment at the precise moment he succeeds in inscribing three exclamation points to punctuate his name. That is, when erratic punctuation, which had wandered outside the text, is finally repatriated, reinscribed in the space of the symbolic.

Beyond any clinic, however, we must pause here over the very possibility of such a "punctuation without a text." Outside the psychoanalytic field, what would a so-called pure or absolute punctuating gesture, that is, one that would not be enrolled in the service of a textual or discursive instance, look like?

We find some beautiful examples of this from the pen of Henri Michaux when, in his experiments with mescaline and other drugs, he listens to music in a singular way. Singular not because his hearing acquired some extraordinary faculty thanks to a state of consciousness profoundly altered by hallucinogenic substances (Michaux insists on this himself, moreover: "There exists a certain banality in the imaginary 'visions' of the world of drugs").[2] Rather, the *banal* singularity of his listening when on mescaline, as he notes it minutely, brings forth the purity of a musical phrasing that frees and detaches itself from words:

> Flown / Sentences without words,* without sounds, without sense . . .
> *What would remain? The rise and fall of the voice (without a voice) or of the expression (but without expression) as when one passes from the high-pitched to the low, from the affirmative to the interrogative, etc. Sentences abstracted from everything except that.[3]

What Michaux can hear under the influence of drugs is thus a phrase without phrase whose movement is all that remains: *phrasing* as such, without semantic or lexical tenor. It is as though the purpose of Michaux's punctuation was to grasp, to capture, the pure beating of this phrasal rhythm, its percussion as it emerges from the withdrawal of meaning. Thus,

> The words that I heard were immediately forgotten, but the way in which they were spoken remained with me. . . . I have often followed a thought. Was it always a thought? At times rather a mental phrase,

mute, signaled, unpronounced, as African tom-toms transmit messages without words. I noted for example: — — . . . .[4]

Michaux seems even to want to set up a veritable punctuating code, a
scale or repertory of signs that would allow him to observe the breaches,
the tears, the lacunae in the symbolic:

> Innumerable holes in the meaning. Then rhythmic interruptions
> in meaning. . . . I had decided (having previously come upon these
> phenomena) that I would mark the holes in meaning with dots, a
> prolonged arrest of meaning with a dash and the end of the arrest
> with another dash further on, that I would mark the arrests of mean-
> ing in depth with two dashes, and finally that when I encountered
> arrests of a grave character (of the kind where you no longer know
> what you are doing) I would nevertheless try to mark them with three
> dashes. (120)[5]

Finally, Michaux inscribes in certain passages, not faults or tears or
longer interruptions or breaks in the symbolic, but pure differences in
quantity, which appear to have resolutely cleared off and freed themselves
from any textual memory or horizon.

> Startling Progression / seizing all sonority / leaving the meaning /
> plunging toward more resonance / toward more / toward more /
> more / More / M O R E /

(86–87)

Michaux thus transcribes the ever-larger gaps in the mesh of meaning with marks that have something decidedly Tristramian about them.
But doing so, he not only inscribes himself in a lineage in which literary
invention goes hand in hand with (typo)graphic invention; he also joins
those rare thinkers who have anticipated the horizon of a general stigmatology through musical listening. In addition to a few considerations
in Adorno,[6] I have in mind most of all Nietzsche: It was not for nothing
that he was the first—we will return to this—to introduce the practice of
auscultation into philosophy.

It is Nietzsche, in fact, who in the course of one of his anti-Wagnerian
diatribes against "the emergence of the actor in music" in *The Case of*

Wagner speaks of "punctuation in music."[7] It is Nietzsche who, taking note of an enlarging, an expansion, of the notion of punctuation toward the field of musical practice, also and at the same time makes it a political issue.

We must read attentively Nietzsche's apparently fleeting and isolated reference to the musicologist Hugo Riemann and his theory of phrasing. We must read it closely, in its immediate context:

> One can grasp it with one's very hands: great success, success with the masses no longer sides with those who are authentic—one has to be an actor to achieve that. . . . In declining cultures, wherever the decision comes to rest with the masses, authenticity becomes super-fluous, disadvantageous, a liability. Only the actor still arouses *great* enthusiasm. Thus, the *golden age* dawns for the actor—for him and for everything related to his kind. Wagner marches with drums and pipes at the head of all artists of delivery, of presentation, of virtuos-ity. . . . The movement Wagner created even reaches over into the field of knowledge: gradually, relevant sciences emerge from centuries of scholasticism. To give an example, I single out for special commenda-tion the merits of *Riemann* regarding rhythmics: he was the first to establish the validity of the central concept of punctuation for music, too (unfortunately, he used an ugly term, *Phrasierung* [phrasing]). (178–79)

Nietzsche's gesture here is formidably complex and ambivalent. And since the stakes are considerable for the very project of a general stigma-tology, it is important to take stock of it, in this context and beyond.

Hugo Riemann, a musicologist, was close to Nietzsche's friend, the composer, pianist, and music critic Carl Fuchs, with whom he collabo-rated on a *Catechism of Phrasing*.[8] Now, what Nietzsche feared, with the introduction of this notion of phrasing into music, is clearly that it would subject the playing of music to an interpretive *diction*, that is, to a *dec-lamation* that always risks becoming histrionic. In short, he feared that music would be subjected to the reign of what Grimarest would call *reci-tation*. But the danger of an invasion of the sphere of music by the theat-ricality of the actor is doubled for Nietzsche by another danger, it too tied to phrasing: that punctuation would make all the minor details equally significant—and thus, in the end, insignificant.

We can understand this better by turning to a letter from Nietzsche to Carl Fuchs that takes up and makes explicit the somewhat cursory argu-ment of *The Case of Wagner*. For the analogy clarified there is this: *Just as* democracy is a decadence that puts decision in the "hands of the masses," *so too* punctuation brings the life of great forms down to the unbounded luxuriance of what is smallest.

Here, then, are the lines that Nietzsche addresses to his friend on 26 August 1888—long, sinuous sentences that I translate as literally as possible, maintaining their incisive meanderings and especially their singular punctuation, for they seem almost to mimic involuntarily the disintegration that they deplore:

> This animation and enlivening of the smallest parts of discourse of music (I wish that you and Riemann would use the words known to everyone from rhetoric: period [sentence], colon, comma, according to the size, likewise interrogatory sentence, conditional sentence, imperative—for the theory of phrasing is definitely the same as punctuation in prose and poetry)—anyway, we considered this animation and enlivening of the smallest parts, as it enters Wagner's practice in music and has spread from there to become almost a dominant system of interpretation (even for actors and singers), with counterparts in other arts—it is a typical symptom of decay, a proof that life has withdrawn from the whole and is luxuriating in the infinitesimal. "Phrasing" would, accordingly, be the symptom of a decline of the organizing power, or, to put it differently, a symptom of incapacity to bridge big areas of relations rhythmically—it would be a decadent form of rhythm.[9]

Although recognizing its importance, Nietzsche thus places the notion of musical punctuation under the sign of this Wagnerism, which for him partakes in a decline, an inexorable erosion. Punctuating amounts to making or letting the infinitesimal proliferate until it sucks the life out of the whole.

I will return at length, *in fine*, to the political dimensions that are inherent in every punctuating gesture in that it always makes a decision. What we must consider for the moment is that, in the sentences of the letter to Fuchs that we have just read, Nietzsche practices precisely this same hyperbolic punctuation whose generalization beyond the textual field he is in the midst of deploring. Now, this is more than a simple and banal contradiction between what one is tempted, too quickly tempted, to call content and expression. What we can hear in this tension is the symptom of an ambivalence, of a stigmatological oscillation between two poles whose names are, respectively, Richard Wagner and Laurence Sterne.

Wagner, we have read, is in effect a name for punctuation as the disintegration and decay of the whole. For Wagner is above all "endless melody," as one of the fragments gathered in the *Assorted Opinions and Maxims* in the second volume of *Human, All Too Human* describes it (§134): a profusion of effects that—in order to avoid at all cost the "petrification, crystallization" of music, that is, its taking form—ends up sounding like "rhythmic paradoxes and blasphemies" (*rhythmische Paradoxien und Lästerreden*), bearing witness in the end to "overripe rhythmic feeling" (*der Überreife des rhythmischen Gefühls*).[10] The hyperpunctuation of Wagnerian phrasing is the becoming-overripe of the rhythmic.

A few pages earlier, in a previous fragment, this same "infinite melody" was nonetheless the emblem of the writer Lorenz (*sic*, for Laurence) Sterne's supreme freedom of spirit. And what this phrase exalts this time, in the author of *Tristram Shandy*, is in fact "an artistic style . . . in which fixed form [*die bestimmte Form*] is constantly being broken up" as well as "displaced" (238): *verschoben*, Nietzsche writes, which is also to say, postponed, adjourned, phased out, deferred. Tristramian overpunctuation would thus be the precise counterpart of, and symmetrical to, Wagnerian hyperpunctuation: its mirror reflection, inflected by a positive sign.

To "an older ear" (*dem älterem Ohre*) Wagner's rhythmic inventions and effects sound like paradoxes, Nietzsche writes in the paragraph of *Assorted Opinions and Maxims* devoted to endless melody (§134). And in fact, the expansion of punctuation beyond the field of writing, the generalization of punctuation without text under the name *phrasing* (*Phrasierung*), is also and perhaps above all a matter of the ear, of listening. But before coming to that, before looking into the Nietzschean figure of *punctuating auscultation* in a moment, and then into the continuation of this figure in Heidegger and Derrida, we must pay attention to a surprising dialogue in which the two anonymous interlocutors seem to gloss, annotate, paraphrase, and initial something that, once again, looks a lot like an infinite melody.

What takes place, then, in this "Conversation on Music" that Nietzsche orchestrates?[11] What happens to the hyperbolic punctuation of Wagnerian phraseology when it is heard, that is, when its declamatory and histrionic theatricality is exposed to acts of listening that punctuate it in turn?

I am going to read closely this singular conversation that Nietzsche might have tuned into between two neighboring auditors in a concert hall just as well as in the hollow of the ear of either one of them. For the dialogue's two voices are at no point identified, given first or last name, attributed. They remain pure instances, abstract places—indicated as A and B—in a field of forces:

A: What do you say to this music?—B: It overwhelmed me, I don't have anything at all to say. Listen! It's beginning all over again!— A: So much the better! Let's see to it that *we* overwhelm it this time. May I accompany this music with a few words? And show you a drama as well that you perhaps did not want to see upon first hearing?—B: Be my guest! I have two ears and more if necessary. Pull up close to me! (174)

A and B are thus letters that mark points describing a triangle. Faced with music, faced with what makes itself heard, they make appear, in the straight line between listening and its object, an angle that diverts, detours, diffracts that line, a gap that makes it possible as address to the other—or from the other. In a more or less Lacanian vein, we could, moreover, describe this structure of address precisely as a punctuation, that is, as the fastening or buttoning of the other in listening.[12]

But the dialogue between A and B from the start also sets the stage for a playback, an echo: This music, B says to A, we are going to play it again (for ourselves) ("it's beginning all over again"); and in this repetition, A adds for B's benefit, an entire theater is getting ready to appear ("a drama as well that you perhaps did not want to see upon first hearing?"). Now, once again, nothing allows us to say if the reprise mentioned is literally that, if it is a true encore, a curtain call at the end of a concert, or if there is, instead, a sort of spectral echo in it that, on the internal scene of each's listening, immediately doubles as its shadow every second that passes. Nothing forbids us from thinking, for example, that B, as in *Fight Club*, could be the Tyler of A, echoing with his uppercuts each instant's auditory sensation; or vice versa, that A could be the "hitter" of B, he who with his slaps and left jabs snaps him back to listening.[13]

What, then, do A and B punctuate with their punchuations? Or better: What phrases, what punctuated phrasings, do they overpunctuate thus? We have already read it: a "drama" that is being prepared. I rewind a bit in order better to listen to it with them:

B: Be my guest! I have two ears and more if necessary. Pull up close to me!—A: —This is not yet what *he* [*il*] wants to say to us, he has only promised up until now that he's going to say something, something unheard of, as his gestures indicate. (174)

(Pause. I hear you asking yourself: Who is *he*? Who is gesticulating thus, *in* the music? We are coming to that. Play.)

How he [*il*]signals with his hand! Pulls himself upright! Waves his arms! . . . How he amplifies his theme! . . . And now he's convinced that he's convinced his listeners, he presents his ideas as if they were the most important things under the sun, he points shamelessly at his theme. . . . What a connoisseur of the soul he is! He holds sway over us with the tricks of a soapbox orator.—But the music has stopped! (174–75)

Taking advantage of an encore that could be the echo that goes along with the music step for step, A, as he anticipated, makes a "drama" appear in it for B. And, during this second listening, which is perhaps only the second listening that each second doubles the first, this strange he or it [*il*] arises in the music.[14]

But who is he, then, this *il* [he or it]?

A is careful never to name him except by this pronoun, the third person singular. Something or someone, in short, that one should perhaps not be in a hurry, after all, to identify trivially with the reassuring figure of the author or composer. For example (even if this is tempting and apparently legitimate) with the histrionic Wagner, who gesticulates, declaims, recites, who punctuates everything with emphasis ("signals with his hand," "waves his arms").

Il [he or it], I would say, in the end leaving him or it essentially undefined, is that which or he who marks events in the flow of music, who dots them. It is the punctuating instance in general, punctuation itself at work, that A and B overpunctuate respectively.[15] And so everything plays out among the three of them—A, B, and *il*—in the ring of their percussions and repercussions. Everything, which is to say, what Nietzsche, through the voice of A, calls "the consciousness of the art of listening."

7 / The Dotted Lines of Auscultation

Écouter (to listen), in French, comes from the Latin verb *auscultare*, which means not only to listen attentively, to lend an ear, but also to give credence to something, to believe in someone, even to listen in on conversations, to watch at the door, or to obey. Most of these ancient meanings still rustle under the pen of Dr. René Théophile Hyacinthe Laënnec when in 1819, in his treatise titled *De l'auscultation médiate* (*On Mediate Auscultation*), he resuscitates the old Latin noun (*auscultatio*) derived from the verb.[1] Seventy years later, seizing on the word's new medical meaning, Nietzsche extends its use to bodies other than that of the patient, to all sorts of bodies (*corps*) or corpora, for example, texts, concepts, values.

This extension, which we will have to be careful not to consider as a simple metaphor, is striking when we hear it in the famous subtitle of *Twilight of the Idols* that, in 1898, mimics the tone of a practical manual: *Wie man mit dem Hammer philosophirt*, "How to Philosophize with the Hammer." This could almost be the title of a medical treatise like Laënnec's, for in his preface Nietzsche does indeed speak of a "cure" (*Genesung*) and of a "curative quality" (*Heilkraft*) when he resolves to "auscultate the idols" (*Götzen aushorchen*).[2]

What, for Nietzsche, calls for such a cure? What must be treated by auscultation?

Strangely, the treatment is not meant for the idols but rather for the doctor himself, for the practitioner who questions them. For what ought to be treated, Nietzsche says literally, is the heaviness, the excess weight, of a punctuation mark. What is to be cured is a question mark whose blackness indicates sickness, threatening the health of the one who handles it, who punctuates with it in order to bring his great project to a successful conclusion: the transformation or transvaluation of values (*Umwerthung aller Werthe*):

> A *revaluation of all values*, this question mark so black, so huge that it casts a shadow on the one who poses it—such a fateful task forces one to run out into the sun at every moment, to shake off a heavy seriousness that has become all too heavy. . . . Another cure . . . is to *auscultate the idols*. . . . To pose questions here with a *hammer* [*mit dem Hammer Fragen stellen*] for once, and maybe to hear in reply that well-known hollow tone that tells of ballooned innards [*jenen berühmten hohlen Ton hören, der von geblähten Einge-weiden redet*]—how delightful for one who has ears even behind his ears [*der Ohren noch hinter den Ohren hat*], for me the old psycholo-gist and pied piper, in whose presence precisely what would like to stay silent *has to speak up*. (3)

An unheard-of scene is being played out here, a scene that *overturns* in so many ways. At the very moment it reaches the field of philosophy, no doubt for the first time, auscultation already announces itself as a treat-ment *for those who question*, as though it could alleviate the repercussions of the question marks one wields.[3] What takes place in the very move-ment of the transvaluation of values is still another overturning: a bend, a turn in which the eye becomes an ear, and even ears, always more ears ("ears even behind his ears"). The initial oppositions that unfold at the heart of the visible—the crepuscular darkness and shadow dispelled by the sun toward which one runs—switch into a repeated series of blows, percussions, and resonances: "As for auscultating idols," Nietzsche con-tinues, "they are not just idols of the age, but *eternal* idols that are touched here with the hammer as with a tuning fork" (*an die hier mit dem Ham-mer wie mit einer Stimmgabel gerührt wird*) (4).

A hollow ring, then, resonating from all directions, once one engages with Nietzsche in such an overturning. The impetus for which—let's not forget, for we will return to this constantly—will have been a magnified printed character, enlarged to the point of becoming monumental and monstrously disturbing: a question mark worthy of those Perekladin saw in his dream.

Before probing the continuations of this auditory turn in Heidegger and Derrida, we must retrace its genealogy from the time of the medical practice of auscultation invented by Laënnec, who inherited it from other earlier techniques for the auditory exploration of the body, as the first edition of his treatise, where he readily acknowledges his debts, shows. First there was his teacher at the Charité de Paris hospital, Jean-Nicolas Corvisart, then the inventor of the so-called percussion method, the Austrian doctor Joseph Leopold Auenbrugger, whose Latin work, which appeared in 1761, Corvisart himself translated in 1808.[4]

In the preface to his new French version, which was accompanied by numerous commentaries, Corvisart is careful to correct an important mistake made in 1770 by Auenbrugger's first translator, a doctor by the name of Rozière de la Chassagne: Percussion, Corvisart affirms, has nothing to do with "succussion," "Hippocrates' method for checking the sound of the chest," which consisted of "shak[ing] the sick, by grasping them by the armpits." Difficult to practice, and even pointless, this succussion, whose description makes us smile today, fell into disuse, whereas percussion for Corvisart has a bright future:

> The method of percussion is founded on the sonorous properties
> of the thoracic cavity in a healthy state. The chest, when struck in a
> particular manner, produces distinct sounds that are comparable to
> one another and that have a perceptible duration, qualities that are
> required in all bodies to produce sound strictly speaking. We will see,
> in the course of this Treatise, how many modifications the sound elicited from the thorax can undergo and what advantage the doctor can
> obtain for knowledge and sometimes even for the cure of the maladies most hidden in the chest. (190F)

Auenbrugger compares this sound to that of "drums [*tympanis*] covered with a thick woolen cloth or other envelope."[5] A muted drum, then, whose resonance, as Corvisart observes, is "extremely variable": In "sanguine" individuals with a "voluminous" heart, for example, "percussion there elicits almost no sound" (193F).

Yet the dullness of the sounds obtained by percussion is in a sense compensated for by the development of the doctor's singular auditory sensibility. Corvisart—who in his commentary goes much further than Auenbrugger on this point—describes this sensibility thus:

> However, such is the point of perfection which can be reached by
> the senses if exercised frequently and properly, and in particular the
> sense of touch, that, even where the author [Auenbrugger] says that a
> fleshy and fatty mass makes the sound dull, the practitioner who has
> studied percussion with precision and diligence experiences, at the

tips of his fingers, a sensation that is equivalent, for him, to the sound an ear can capture. (194F)

The practitioner here seems literally to listen *with the tips of his fingers*.[6] This, then, is the *digital* method that Laënnec inherits from Auenbrugger, via the translation and commentary of his teacher, Corvisart. He commends it as "one of the most valuable discoveries ever made in medicine" (3F) while also recognizing its defects, or rather its limits: It is incapable of locating the signs of many ailments; it often gives "equivocal" results; and, most of all, it demands a "dexterity that many men cannot acquire" (5F). In sum, Laënnec writes, mediate auscultation "must not make us forget [the method] of Avenbrugger [*sic*]; on the contrary, the latter acquires quite a fresh degree of value through the simultaneous employment, and becomes applicable in many cases, wherein its solitary application is either useless or harmful" (13F; 7–8E).[7] Auscultation will therefore not come to *replace* percussion, substituting itself for it; rather, it will extend it by *generalizing* it beyond its limits.

To be sure, as Laënnec never stops insisting, from now on it will be a question of *mediate* auscultation by means of an auditory prosthesis, the stethoscope, which keeps the ear at a distance from direct contact with the body.[8] But in the end something remains, even transposed in the distance, of the punctiform tactility of percussion: Even without touching it immediately, even without sticking his ear to it, the one who auscultates the body penetrates and even pierces it, marks it, and examines it as an *auditory corpus*. And does this by *posing questions* to the hollow cavity Auenbrugger compared to "barrels that, when they are empty, resonate at all points; but that, full, lose even more sound than they gave, since the volume of air they contained has been diminished" (*Nouvelle Methode*, 205).

Practicing the digital striking of percussion and then listening to the repercussions of his auscultation, the doctor who questions the body *solicits* it. He will hear what he will have been able to make resonate, what will have arisen in the ringing made by his strike, in the reverberation or echo of his questioning gesture.[9] But what the medical ear awaits by way of response is not only a listening combined with touching, it is also a *vision*. Tactile listening alone would not suffice in the practice of auscultation. Hearing there is a deferred look; it is but a sort of relay between what the eyes cannot observe inside the closed interior of the body and what they must nevertheless end up seeing: "It is necessary," Laënnec writes, "to have occasionally verified, by autopsy, the diagnosis established by means of the cylinder [of the stethoscope], in order that we may acquire confidence in the instrument and in our own observation, and that we may be convinced, by ocular demonstration, of the correctness of the indications obtained" (14F; 8E). Observations of this sort abound in Laënnec's treatise: "I have been able to verify by autopsy that I had been correct" (18); "I noticed this fact several times in an autopsy" (350); "I have not yet been able to verify this conjecture sufficiently by autopsy" (383). In short, the auditory punctuation of questioning percussion always *awaits* the focal clarification that necropsy will bring: As Michel Foucault puts it so well, it is a question of "drawing *in dotted lines* the future autopsy."[10]

In order to grasp the singularity of this medical listening whose paradigm we will soon see extend to the field of philosophy, we would have to lend it an ear *in the interval*: We would have to listen to it listen *in the between* in which it is suspended, between a direct touching that it already no longer is and a seeing to come that it is not yet. What would appear then, in this suspension of listening between touch and gaze, is this: If percussion is a *dotting* of the body, auscultation is an *overpunctuation*: What striking localized with the tips of the fingers, overpunctuation divides yet again.

As Laënnec explains, it is indeed a question of discerning—by listening—*more than one sign at one point*. One must know how to discriminate, how to differentiate in the depth of the body, by punctuating again and again what appears in the stigmatic unity of one and the same point on its surface. Thus, one reads in the 1828 republication of the *Treatise on Mediate Auscultation*:

> After a month or two of practice, the ear grows accustomed to distinguishing, in the midst of noises that come to it all at once, the one it is looking for, and to hearing it exclusively, in a sense, even when it is weaker than all the others. Every day during clinical visits I hear *in the same point*, the heartbeat, breathing, various rattles, intestinal rumblings, and I listen to and study each of these sounds successively, I notice at the same time a muscular noise produced by the patient or me; and although several of the students around me are walking or speaking in a low voice at the same moment, I rarely have to ask for silence. (23)

When he later describes some "quavering" that indicates a certain ailment of the lungs, Laënnec's auditory overpunctuation seems at times to proceed in the mode of echolocation, like certain animals such as dolphins or bats. For it divides the punctiform instant into a plurality or stacking of points in space:

> One hears *separately, though in the same instant,* the resonating voice and the quavering and argentine resounding, such that the latter seems to be made in a point a bit further away or closer to the observer's ear than the resonance of the voice. (34, my emphasis)

One understands then that, in one point, an entire world of points can arise. A universe of punctiform cracklings, pointillist clouds that Laënnec tries to fix with a vocabulary that he admits he has to borrow in part from the visible:

> The mucous rhonchus, listened to with the help of the stethoscope, presents many varieties of character that are easier to recognize than they are to analyze and especially to describe, and of which we can only form a notion by comparing the perceptions derived from the sense of hearing with such as sight might offer. In listening to it we receive the impression of bubbles, such as are produced by blowing through a pipe into soapy water. The ear seems to appreciate most distinctly the consistence of the fluid which forms the bubbles. . . . It recognizes in no less certain a manner the variable volume of these bubbles and, in this respect, we can say that the rhonchus is *very large, large, medium, small,* or *minute.* The last term is particularly fitting for the crepitous rhonchus as it is observed in first-degree peripneumonia, in which it seems that a multitude of small equal-sized bubbles form at once and vibrate, rather than boil, on the surface of a fluid. Mucous rhonchus, on the contrary, appears always larger and most often unequal in size, so as to convey, *in the same point and in the same moment* [my emphasis], the idea of a liquid into which one is blowing and which forms bubbles, some the size of a filbert, others only as large as a cherry-stone hempseed. We can estimate quite exactly the quantity of bubbles. . . . It sometimes seems that the point of lung beneath the stethoscope is filled with bubbles that touch each other; and at other times there seems to be only one here and there, at a distance from one another. . . . Often one hears a bubble being formed alone from time to time, while the intervening portion of lung yields the simple sound of respiration or no sound at all, as the case may be. When the

mucous rhonchus is very large and infrequent, we can distinctively perceive the bubbles form and burst. When it exists at once copious, large, and constant, it is sometimes so noisy as to resemble the rolling of a drum. (45–46F; 50–51E)

An entire *chronicle of the bubble* is sketched out here. A dynamic or genetic description of the points that appear and proliferate in a single point: that are born, grow, burst, disappear, and regenerate.

Points against points: The oscillating eardrum of the mediate auscultator, equipped with his stethoscope, gathers answers to the questions with which he interrogates and strikes the vibrating body. With words he borrows in advance from the register of the visible in medical knowledge, he sends probing blows, he opens, drills [*fore*], or perforates [*perfore*] the dotted bodily surface in order to overpunctuate it by digging into it an otographic volumetry in which countless points within points bubble. Thus becoming hyperpoints, inflated and animated by an internal dissemination, the points foam. Or better, as Raymond Queneau said so well: They *bulbulate*.[11]

8 / Monauralisms, or The Bubble of Quotation Marks

"To tympanize—philosophy": With this injunction, Derrida in 1972 opened the discourse of *Margins of Philosophy*. An injunction echoed, two pages later, by this watchword borrowed directly from Nietzsche: "To philosophize with a hammer."[1]

To tympanize (from the Greek *tumpanon*, "drum," from which the verb *tumpanizein*, "to beat a drum," is derived) first of all means to criticize or ridicule publicly, which was done in the past by accompanying legal decisions and judgments with drumming. To tympanize then means to tire, trouble, bother by deafening the tympan in the ear. Finally, to tympanize means to inflate or bloat the abdomen, stretching it tight with internal air pressure, like the skin of timpani. All these meanings are there, on the lookout, as it were, ready to jump out suddenly, lurking in the opening of *Margins*, which Derrida punctuates with the long dash that, like Tristram, he too uses and abuses, though no doubt for different reasons: "To tympanize—philosophy" is not only to attack it publicly, to torment it, but also to auscultate or percuss it by listening in order, as Nietzsche said of the idols, to "to hear in reply that well-known hollow tone that tells of ballooned innards."[2]

Derrida soon adds yet another sense to the broad scope of the verb "to tympanize" (and we don't really know whether its object is philosophy or if philosophy, in apposition to "tympanize" by way of a silent dash, is tympanization itself), allowing it to drift toward its homonym in the typographical lexicon: "In terms of the printing press," he asks, "what is a tympan?" (xxv). And before quoting a "treatise on typography" (xxvi) at length, he responds:

In terms of the manual printing press, then, there is not one tympan but several. Two frameworks, of different material, generally wood and iron, fit into one another, are lodged, if one can put it thus, in one another. One tympan in the other, one of wood the other of iron, one large and one small. Between them, the sheet of paper [*feuille*]. (xxvi)

Now, we know that *feuille* is French slang for *ear*.[3] So we are led to read this allusion to the traditional art of printing as an allegory for the auditory apparatus as a mechanism for inscription or marking. As a result, the vocabulary of typography is superimposed, as it were, onto the vocabulary of hearing, as though some structural affinity brought the mechanism of the ear together with what is most silent in the typographic mark, with the muffled beats of what remains unheard.

Which is to say with what Derrida will later in *Margins* describe as a sort of archepunctuation that would silently space the text as well as language and speech—in short, the very play of différ^e/$_a$nce:

So-called phonetic writing . . . can function only by admitting into its system nonphonetic "signs" (punctuation, spacing, etc.). And an examination of the structure and necessity of these nonphonetic signs quickly reveals that they can barely tolerate the concept of the sign itself. Better, the play of difference, which, as Saussure reminded us, is the condition for the possibility and functioning of every sign, is in itself a silent play. Inaudible is the difference between two phonemes which alone permits them to be and to operate as such. The inaudible opens up the apprehension of two present phonemes such as they present themselves. (5)

Before *Margins*, in *Of Grammatology*, Derrida already attached great significance to this punctuation, which he said is "the best example of a nonphonetic mark within writing."[4] And later he will continue to pay meticulous and intrigued attention to punctuation marks, sometimes going so far as to depict them as actual characters, like the fiery periods and exclamation points that haunt Perekladin's dreams.

And so, for example, in *Of Spirit* we will see quotation marks that "provide . . . surveillance around the word,"[5] which as a result finds itself "contained at the doorstep or held at the frontier" (29) and even half hidden, withdrawn behind a veil:

It's the law of quotation marks. Two by two they stand guard: at the frontier or before the door, assigned to the threshold in any case, and these places are always dramatic. The apparatus lends itself to theatricalization, and also to the hallucination of the stage and its machinery: two pairs of pegs hold in suspension a sort of drape, a veil or a curtain. Not closed, just slightly open. (31)

We should not, however, be in a rush to conclude that this theatricality, this staged character of quotation marks, is at work in the realm of the visible. Like other punctuation marks, quotation marks are inaudible and cannot be vocalized per se: We don't hear quotation marks themselves, as such, only in the effect their intonation has on other signs, in the differences they imprint on the pronunciation of the words they surround and demarcate.[6] Silent yet producing *differences in tone*, quotation marks are also—or at least they can be—*invisible*, as Derrida regularly emphasizes when he chases after them, when he tries to flush them out precisely where they cannot be seen.

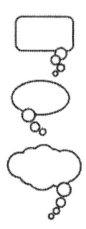

It is a question, then, of listening to these punctuation marks that are always liable to recede from view, of lending an ear, sounding out, percussing, and auscultating the text like Laënnec listening to the body of his patient—to get in response the bulbulating of all the voices that rustle within it. Even more than the pegs that hold up a curtain inflated by a ghostly presence, quotation marks are the bubbles that, as Proust puts it so well in *Du côté de chez Swann* [*Swann's Way*], "isolate" the word.[7]

And these bubbles abound; they proliferate, even, and especially when we do not see them. "Once quotation marks demand to appear," Derrida writes in *Parages*, "they don't know where to stop" (104).

Speaking of his "hermit philosophy" (*Einsiedler-Philosophie*), in a posthumous fragment from June–July 1885, Nietzsche noted that "even if it had been written with a lion's claw" (*mit einer Löwenklaue geschrieben*), it would nonetheless "always look like a philosophy of 'goose feet'" (*eine Philosophie der "Gänsefüßchen"*).[8] That is—for this is what the German word means—a philosophy of "quotation marks" (between quotation marks).

Contrary to what such an image might lead us to believe—a "weak" philosophy as opposed to a "strong" one, an uncertain or unstable philosophy rather than one that is thetic and sure of itself—it is important to assert, with and perhaps even beyond Nietzsche, that to philosophize with quotation marks is in fact to philosophize with a hammer, that is, *to think in punchuation*. Put differently, it is to raise, emphasize, and amplify the gaps in tones and intonations, this "tonal difference" that, as Derrida recalls, an entire tradition dreamed of effacing in "the atonal norm of philosophic allocution."[9]

In addition to quotation marks, auscultation requires italics as a sort of percussive correlate that completes quotation marks: not, however, the underlining so many authors abuse, as though every one of their words were to be introduced with fanfare, with drums and cymbals, like Wagner, whose prose Nietzsche mocked in a posthumous fragment from the summer of 1875 ("everything is so important to him, as though everything ought to be underlined," he notes, putting his finger once again on Wagner's tendency to punctuate hyperbolically). Rather, I'm referring to the use of italics in those great scenes of philosophic stethoscopy, such as, for example, Heidegger's *The Principle of Reason* and Derrida's *Politics of Friendship*.

Heidegger, at the end of the fifth session of what was first a course offered at the University of Freiburg in 1955–56, thus orchestrates a masterly overturning, a striking reversal, in the reading of the principle of reason as Leibniz formulated it (*nihil est sine ratione*, "nothing is without reason"). Thanks to a new intonation that displaces the punctuating percussion, Heidegger makes Leibniz's phrase resonate differently, he *phrases* it differently, playing with the italics to make heard what to that point had remained inaudible:

> We should now tune in to how, in this sentence which speaks in a hollow unison [*gleichtönig*], two different tonalities vibrate [*zwei verschiedene Tonarten schwingen*]. We can say: "*Nihil* est *sine* ratione." "*Nothing* is *without* reason." In the affirmative form this means: everything has a reason. Yet we can also set the pitch in this way: "Nihil *est* sine *ratione*." "Nothing *is* without *reason*." In the affirmative form this means: every *being* (*as a being*) has a *reason*.[10]

For his part, Derrida, in what was initially the first session of a seminar he offered in 1988–89, seems to echo this accentual mark around which *Der Satz vom Grund* turns. For what he stages there too is a change in intonation that affects the meaning of the Greek sentence *ō philoi, oudeis philos* ("O my friends, there is no friend," in Montaigne's translation, who attributes the phrase to Aristotle). The initial *omega*, Derrida explains, can be written "without an accent . . . without an iota subscript and without a breathing," so that we understand it as a vocative interjection ("ô amis," *ō philoi*).[11] And this is the generally accepted reading. But with a barely audible diacritical change, the *omega* can be transcribed with a rough breathing and an iota subscript, thus becoming a pronominal dative ("for he who has friends," *hoi philoi*). And this *coup d'accent* causes a reversal in how the phrase is heard: "He who has too many friends has none," Derrida then translates, noting that "it all comes down to less than a letter, to the difference of a breath" (209).

Beyond the contextual reasons that lead Heidegger and Derrida, in the wake of Nietzsche, to probe a given text or phrase in the philosophical tradition, what we must pause over is their very gesture, which, with a punctuating blow, brings out differences in tone where, on first reading, there were none. Where then do these differences come from? From where do these jumps in intonation emerge? Just as a certain "Conversation on Music" between A and B taught us, they can proceed only from the triangulation of a listening that is itself *differential*, that is, already divided, as Derrida writes in the essay that concludes the original French edition of *Politics of Friendship*, between "more than one ear" and "more than an ear."[12] To bring out these tonal gaps or spacings, to put *différance* to work in the auscultation of the text or discourse, supposes that every step, every instant, every mark is doubled or restitched by the other, re-marked or overpunctuated by the other ear or the ear of the other.

It is not by accident that *Politics of Friendship* closes with a study of "Heidegger's Ear," wherein one of the persistent questions concerns the structurally *binaural* character of listening, divided between two tympana. To be sure, this concern is not new in Derrida, who already alluded, here and there, to auditory stereophony in philosophic listening.[13] But what is at stake in the distance or distension between ears that do not form a pair becomes central and thematized as such in the deconstructive analysis to which he submits Heideggerian otology, as the following passage, among many others, testifies:

> Heidegger's ear then divides itself. More precisely, it is divided in two. There is a deaf ear like that of everyone today. . . . The other ear overhears the unheard through the deafness. (184)

One can easily think of this in terms of an animal, one that can thus point its auricles in different directions. And indeed, by questioning the Heideggerian discourse on animality Derrida also interrogates his *monaural* definition of listening in man,[14] which is thus essentially called to gather, to collect, itself: Citing the statement in *Logos*, Heidegger's 1951 lecture on Heraclitus's fragment 50, according to which "we hear when we are all ear" (*wir hören wenn wir ganz Ohr sind*), Derrida emphasizes and criticizes—he *tympanizes*, one might say—the "movement from the plural or the dual to the singular" (188), a movement in which the logocentrism of listening is lodged.

However, even if he has been more attentive than anyone to what is at stake in such a movement, Derrida seems to relativize its import *for the ear*:

> Here we are dealing with the same schema that permitted distinguishing Dasein's hand, always engaged with speaking and λόγος, from the ape's prehensile organs (yet with this essential difference: one can separate the two hands, and speaking of "the" hand isn't self-evident, while one cannot in the same way separate the act of listening according to the two ears).

This parenthesis is strange and rather enigmatic,[15] coming after Derrida's meticulous and prudent reading of the "internal ear," this "inner ear" (*innere Ohr*) that Heidegger makes a point of distinguishing from the "sensory or sensible ear." Is the "essential difference" that this somewhat cursory phrase refers to—the difference between manual manipulation and listening as duality—a straightforward sensible difference? Does it stem from the *fact* that physically the ears listen *together* as long as one is not plugged? And if not, why couldn't the two ears be separated?

What makes Derrida hesitate? Where does this precaution, which seems to restrain and limit the scope of his deconstruction of Heideggerian *monaurality*, come from?

It is as if Derrida had stopped on the threshold of a phenomenon that should have interested him to the highest degree, well beyond its anthropological or zoological empiricism: that is, the discriminating faculty that we call *echolocation*, which, in both animals and humans, resides in the gap between the two tympana. In the animal world, bats are virtuosos of

this topographical use of the binaural, which allows them to locate with infinite precision an object on the otoroute of sounds, through the echo of their calls, returned from the target with a slight *interaural* discrepancy, from one ear to the other. In humans, some blind people have become famous for developing a similar technique. This was the case, it is said, of the blind traveler James Holman, who managed to roam the world until his death in 1857. And it is also the case of the superhero Daredevil depicted in the eponymous comic published by Marvel beginning in 1964: After losing his sight in an accident, Matt Murdock, to use his real name, compensates for his handicap by developing his own particular way of punctuating or percussing his environment, collecting in return echoes that allow him to detect everything that happens within it.

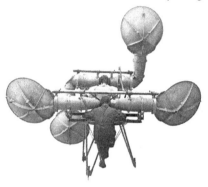

The art of military listening was not to be outdone, of course; the technique of echolocation peaked with a piece of equipment whose golden age ended with the invention of modern radar and sonar. Medical auscultation has similarly made use of the gap between the ears: Beginning in 1850, Laënnec's monaural stethoscope was gradually replaced by a binaural model. And toward the middle of the nineteenth century, there were "differential stethoscopes" whose merits a Scottish medical review from 1873 praised in these terms: "By allowing us virtually to place each ear on a different part of the chest at the same time, it enables us to differentiate sound easily." As Jonathan Sterne quite rightly notes in citing this description,[16] such an auditory prosthesis, whose use was never really generalized subsequently, nonetheless testifies, with its nascent stereophonic effect, to the concern for echolocation inherent in the practice of medical listening. This was already implied, moreover, by Laënnec's remark that he heard two sonorous events or signs "separately, although at the same instant . . . in a point a bit more distant from or closer to the observer's ear."

One could say that this echographic auscultation that penetrates the interior of bodies or spaces is the paradigm of listening as clearing a path [*frayage*]. It is like the opening of a gallery or tunnel that, starting from a point that is struck, leads into the thickness of a blind area where more or less cavernous bubbles await here and there. The surveying strike causes the cavities to resonate in order to "hear in response that famous hollow sound" that the philosopher with a hammer called to mind in putting his ear up to the idols. This is why, as I have insisted elsewhere, the topology that opens itself to listening is also a *topmology* [*taupologie*];[17] it results from that burrowing that the verb *heraushören* used by Heidegger in his 1940 text on Nietzsche describes so well. The French version renders this weakly with "perceive" (and the English with "detect"), where it should almost (to force language somewhat) translate literally as *exlisten* to mark clearly that it is a question of a true *excavation by listening*.[18]

And yet at its auscultating tip, at the stigmatic extremity of its homing device, where it bores and perforates [*fore et perfore*] by tympanizing, listening proceeds by gathering the *difference between two repercussions*. And if we had to give it a figure, it would be a *double point* that, unlike the colon (in French, *deux points*), would not have the quality of a re-collection [*recueillement*] that brings the two parts together. Thus, it would not be a typographic synonym of equality[19] but rather the mark of a *between-two-punctuations*, a sort of instantaneous interval that opens the possibility of all the angles, all the triangulations, in which listening can take place.

What to do, then, with the parenthesis of "Heidegger's Ear" we considered earlier? How to understand this parenthesis that states that "one can separate the two hands, and speaking of 'the' hand isn't self-evident, while one cannot in the same way separate the act of listening according to the two ears"? The only way to understand it, I believe, is this: Precisely because it is structurally binaural, listening—or auscultation—can play out only in the gap between two ears, which therefore means that they cannot *simply* be disjointed or separate.

One might say, playing on another Derrida title, that there is never any *monauralism* except of the other.[20] Accordingly, auscultating otography, in its oscillating beat between two tympana, strikes with punchuations, each one reverberating in doubling itself. Listening thus opens its path by following the fine line that takes it from percussions to repercussions. And this rhythm of ours—a sort of structural jump or burst that immediately restitches every step, move, or mark into an angulated playback—I have consistently described as an *overpunctuation*; and we must now try to understand its general logic.

The overpunctuating beat that simulates the tympanic blow—returned either from the other ear or the ear of the other—immediately splits, forming the two foci of an ellipsis, of an invisible bubble:

«   »

9 / *Punctum Saliens,* or The Pulsating Point

To try to understand better what we have repeatedly identified as a sort of overpunctuating jolt that animates punctuation marks, let us first turn to an apparently simple figure of the point: this point • as Hegel describes it in the first chapter of his *Phenomenology of Spirit*, which takes up the here and now of sense certainty.

"The here that is meant," Hegel writes, "would be the point" (*das Hier, das gemeint wird, wäre der Punkt*).[1] It *would* be, yes, except that, in reality, "it *is* not" (*er ist aber nicht*). And if it is not, it is because, "when it is pointed out as something that is" (*indem er als seiend aufgezeigt wird*), it is showing itself, it is "pointing out [that] shows itself" (*zeigt sich das Aufzeigen*). Showing or pointing out shows *itself*, in fact, as what *it* is: "not immediate knowing" (*nicht unmittelbares Wissen*) but a signing, an indication, a reference, in short, a "movement [*Bewegung*] from the Here that is meant and through many Heres [*durch viele Hier*] into the universal Here [*in das allgemeine Hier*]." The fact of pointing out a here, Hegel says in short, this pointing returns in a sense upon itself; it points itself out as that which designates only the empty generality of any here whatsoever, which could be this here here just as well as that one there.

In fact, in this place where I am now writing these lines, in this garden I am sitting in, I can say, as does Hegel:

> "Here" is, e.g., the tree. [But] if I turn round, this truth has vanished and is converted into its opposite: "No tree is here, but a house instead." (60–61)

In its generality, the here is thus "a simple plurality of heres" (*eine einfache Vielheit der Hier*). And likewise, the now is "a simple plurality of nows" (*eine einfache Vielheit der Iztz*):

> To the question, "What is Now?," let us answer, e.g. "Now is night." In order to test the truth of this sense-certainty a simple experiment will suffice. We write down this truth; a truth cannot lose anything  by being written down, any more than it can lose anything through our preserving it. If *now, this noon,* we look again at the written truth we shall have to say that it has become stale. (60)

Like the here, the now that we believed we could point to as unique, all in one point, this now is not one; in the end it is several. Its punctiformity explodes into a plurality; it splits precisely when it is pointed to, when it is shown in its unicity and supposed identity, as if it were precisely showing it that made it break into pieces.

This moment of the bursting of the point is what we have attempted to define (in the Lacanian button point as in Tristram's autobiography, in the three exclamation points that nail down Perekladin's signature as in the markings of the Egyptian scribes verifying their accounts, in the initials of an Asterius or a Symmachus, in the conversation between A and B as in the auscultating otography inaugurated by Nietzsche). And now we find it again at the pointy end, as it were, of the gesture of deixis, when in Hegel indicating indicates itself, showing shows itself (*zeigt sich das Aufzeigen*).

In fact, if the here loses its unified and singular—its atomystic, Derrida would say—punctiformity once it is pointed out, if it explodes from the blow of pointing, of its *deixis*, shattering into raindrops of heres, this is not only because the here becomes iterable, capable of being repeated from this here to that one. It is also because the index that points to it in a sense returns upon itself; it rebounds from what it points to, sending its pointing back toward itself, *overpointing* itself.

There is in this movement, to which we will constantly return, the outline of a rhythm, an overpunctuating pulsation, that we will also find throughout that other great stigmatological fable that Hegel's *Philosophy of Nature* is in so many ways. For there we see the figure of the point appear *doubly* at each great stage in the construction of the world: on the one hand, as an element that is always crucial to the development of the concept of nature that leads from inert matter to life, and on the other, in a rebound or jump to which we are now going to listen attentively, as the punctuation of the narrative itself, as the punctuating phrasing of the story that recounts this development. We will thus hear the point at work on two levels at once: It will be one of the protagonists *in* the story at the same time that it is the rhythm *of* this story (were we to show this Hegelian discourse like a film, we could say that the point will play an at once diegetic and metadiegetic role in it).

In fact, after an introduction to the "concept of nature" in general, the *Philosophy of Nature* almost immediately concentrates, in the "Mechanics," on space and time. That is, on the point. For according to Hegel, nature, as it first presents itself simply as a mechanism, is the indeterminate continuity of space in which one finds heres side by side and totally indifferent to one another; that is, the difference between this here and that one is not a difference. The result being that space, which seems to be formed of points, which appears as a sort of dotted line stretching to infinity in all directions, is in reality perfectly continuous.[2]

The truth of the point, Hegel says in short, will not be found in space. For if, as he affirms, the point is essentially an interruption (*Unterbrechung*), this interruption cannot take place in the simple indifferent continuity of spatiality. The real force of the point would not be spatial insofar as, in space, there is no end point ("no Here is ultimate" [*kein Hier ein Letztes ist*], 29). The true effect of punctuation will take place, therefore, in time: "In time the point thus has actuality" (*in der Zeit hat der Punkt also Wirklichkeit*, addendum to §257).

We will consider the implications of the fact that punctuation has actuality in time after having auscultated a certain pulsating beat of the point. Which, moreover, is explicitly formulated as such by Hegel when he notes, in the margin of one of the Jena manuscripts that prefigure the *Philosophy of Nature*, that time is *der springende Punkt*.[3] Difficult to render in French, this German expression is modeled on the Latin *punctum saliens*, which in the vocabulary of physiology designates the embryonic heart of a living being. William Harvey, who is credited with the discovery of the circulation of blood, thus speaks, in his 1651 *Exercitationes de generatione animalium* of the *punctum sanguineum saliens*, of this "pulsating point the color of blood" that appears in a chicken's egg from the fourth day on. And he describes the pulsation of this point in these terms:

In its diastole, it shines like a small spark of fire [*ceu minima ignis scintillula, effulgeat*]; and immediately after, in its systole, it completely escapes view and disappears.[4]

The *punctum saliens*, that is, Hegel's *springende Punkt*, is thus a leaping, springing, or hopping point. A flashing point that appears and disappears, that pulsates and jumps.

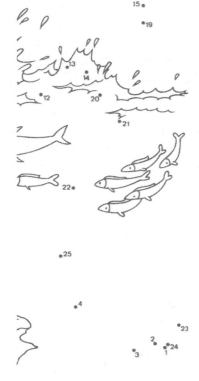

At the beginning of the final section of the *Philosophy of Nature*, which is devoted to "Organics," Hegel describes the appearance of "points of life" (*Lebenspunkte*), that is, of what he names, in the addendum to this same paragraph (§341), "living points" (*lebendige Punkte*) produced by a "punctiform development [a becoming-point, then] of vitality in the living" (*Punktualisierung der Lebendigkeit zum Lebendigen*). And it is in the sea par excellence, it is in the marine element, that this living punctiformity spreads in a rhythm that prefigures what will be the pulsation of the *punctum saliens* in the animal:

The sea itself is . . . a living process which is always on the point [*immer auf der Sprunge steht*: literally, is ready to jump or spring] of breaking forth into life [*in Leben auszubrechen*] but again perpetually falls back into water [*ins Wasser zuruckfällt*] because this contains all the moments of that process: the point of the subject [*den Punkt des Subjekts*], neutrality, and the dissolution of this subject into neutrality. (296)

In the sea, life emerges at every point [*point en tout point*]; it appears and disappears constantly; it never stops emerging and stopping in order to fall (back) into the water.

With the plant, life in Hegel's eyes is no longer content to flicker thus by peeking through only to dissolve immediately into a sort of primordial soup. For, as the addendum to §342 puts it, "The organic begins . . . where vitality draws itself together into a point [*die Lebendigkeit sich in einen Punkt zusammennimmt*]; this point maintains and produces itself [*sich erhält und sich produziert*], pushes itself away from itself [*sich von sich abstösst*] and gives birth to new points." But the organic "subjectivity" that Hegel describes as "punctiform" (*punktuelle*, addendum to §337) still remains "brittle" (*spröd*): Which is to say that, by differentiating itself, by dividing itself in its unity, the organic being is "torn out of itself" (*ausser sich gerissen*). It does not become other by taking hold of itself in itself, but bursts into "an infinite number of subjects": "Leaves, roots, the stem are also only individuals" and not limbs, as will be the case in the animal organism (§350 and following), the culminating point of the "Organics" and of the *Philosophy of Nature* as a whole.[5]

While the plant thus has not yet taken back into itself the external-ity of the points that it itself nevertheless already engenders, the animal "conserves itself in its being-other." That is, in the animal, in its animated animation, "spatial asunderness is sublated in the soul [*ist in der Seele das Aussereinander des Raumes aufgehoben*]" (addendum to §339 [p. 278]). In this sense, the animal is no longer a simple punctiform self that breaks in producing a multitude of other points, like the plant does. It is a self that continuously takes itself back into itself; it is a self *that reaffirms itself* as self. Hegel says this literally in the nearly stuttering repetition of the word *Selbst*, which, doubled, marks what he calls the "absolutely characteristic feature of the animal" (addendum to §351 [p. 353]):

> This punctiformity, which yet is infinitely determinable [*dieses Punk-tuelle und doch unendlich Bestimmbare*] . . . because it has itself for its object, is the subject as self-self [*das Subjekt als Selbst-Selbst*], as self-feeling [*Selbstgefühl*]. (353)

To say that the animal is a self-self is of course to mark, on the one hand, that its reiterated ipseity is stronger and higher than that of the plant; but it is also, on the other hand, to imply that its ipseity is in a sense stuttering, and even infinitely stammering. That it is neither stable nor given nor fixed but open to the flickering of its becoming. In the end, the animal is what Hegel describes a few paragraphs later as "the *pulsating point* of selfhood" (*dem* springenden Punkt *der Selbstheit*): More than a simple punctiform or stigmatic ipseity, it would be the ipsological pulsat-ing of the self.[6]

In short, not only does the animal have, possess, or contain in itself this *punctum saliens* that physiology deals with and to which Hegel al-ludes in the addendum to §354 when he speaks of the heart and the circulation of blood; but also and especially, it *is* itself, as self-self, this pulsating point where ipseity constitutes itself by deposing and recon-stituting itself endlessly. If, in the animal, punctiformity, the punctiform character of the self, no longer breaks apart (in fact, the animal *dies*, it begins to *be able to die*, which is not the case of the plant), if the point is no longer external to itself but begins to pulsate or beat to the rhythm of the life that feels itself living, it is because the point here takes itself as its object: *The point punctuates itself*, one might say, in the animated animal.

10 / The Point of the Overcast Stitch

But I have gone a bit quickly. Before the emergence of the "points of life" in the "Organics," there are other kinds of punctiformity at work in Hegel's *Philosophy of Nature*. Even if they are admittedly less obvious, even if they do not spring or leap immediately into view, we must pay attention to them.

Thus, before the appearance of the *punctum saliens* of emergent life, there is the moment (§295–302) in which the logic of nature—the unfolding of its concept—produces what Hegel calls cohesion (*Kohäsion*). Which is to say that matter, "resisting the pressure and thrust of external force," finds the manner proper to it of yielding, bending, or breaking, thus of "showing itself to be independent in its form" (§296, 131). In short, matter has a bearing, a holding-together (*Zusammenhalt*) within which one can distinguish different modalities: brittleness (*Sprödigkeit*) or, inversely, elasticity or malleability (*Dehnbarkeit, Hämmerbarkeit*). Now, in opposition to the latter, which is literally a propensity to become a surface or plane (*Flächenhaftigkeit*, the German text says), the tendency to break is described as a "punctiformity" (*Punktualität*)[1] whose surpassing or sublation is elasticity, which Hegel describes as the becoming-central of *every point* (addendum to §298):

> Elasticity is the retreat of a body into itself [*die Elastizität ist das Zurückgehen in sich selbst*] so as immediately to reinstate itself [*unmittelbar wiederherzustellen*]. The cohesive body when struck, pushed, or pressed by another body suffers a negation of its material being as occupying space, and so of its occupation of a particular

place [*so wird seine Materialität als raumeinnehmend und somit seine Örtlichkeit negiert*]. We are thus in the presence of the negation of material asunderness [*des materiellen Aussereinander*], but equally, too, of the negation of this negation, of the reinstatement of materiality [*das Wiederherstellen der Materialität*]. . . . Each particle of cohesive matter thus behaves as a center [*als Mittelpunkt*]. (135–56)

What is announced here, in the description of elasticity, is already a sort of *punctum saliens* before the fact, a point that pulsates or leaps even before there is animal life. When matter becomes elastic, then, the punctiformity of the point is no longer, as at the beginning of the *Philosophy of Nature*, a simple break (*Unterbrechung*) that arrests and ruptures: It obeys the movement of pulsating overpunctuation in which the abrupt interruption is itself interrupted. As a result, the point here rises up, projects, overcoming itself in a leap that removes its brittle immediacy and gives it the suppleness—elasticity, precisely—of an expansion and multiplication of itself. This, in short, is what Hegel also describes as the oscillation (*Erzittern*) or vibration (*Schwingen*) of the body in itself (§299 and addendum). An oscillation that, seen from another angle—no longer in itself but from the outside—is named sound (*Klang*).

What, then, is sound in the *Philosophy of Nature*? And how is sound related to the punctuating and pulsating life of the point?

Hegel describes sonorous vibration in a long sentence [*période*]. His sentence is itself oscillating, full of nodes and antinodes, one might say, to borrow the vocabulary of vibratory acoustics. I will try to translate as literally as possible this sentence, which seems to mimic, in its overpunctuated syntax, the very thing it seeks to say: sonorous form, Hegel writes,[2] takes place

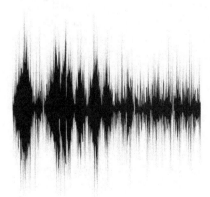

in the *vibration* of the material body—i.e. through the momentary negation of its parts and, equally, the negation of this negation of them, the two negations being so linked that one evokes the other, and through an oscillation between the subsistence and the negation of specific gravity and cohesion—this simple form . . . achieves . . . mechanically soul-like manifestation. (137)

Sound thus frees itself of matter while constantly returning to it (it is, Hegel says in the addendum to this same paragraph, "freedom *from* heavy matter which is at the same time *in* heavy matter" [138]). It completes in matter what elasticity had already introduced to it: an oscillation from self to self. In short, sound, which is like a "mechanical light" (*gleichsam das mechanische Licht*), is a sort of *stroboscopic* self, a pulsed and pulsating self that vibrates in the very negation of materiality, which has always started over again.

The description of vibration we have just read also holds, of course, for voice, that particular kind of sound produced when that which makes the vibrating body vibrate is the body itself. Just like sound, voice is thus that vibration of the body that results from the elasticity that distances it from, and brings it closer to, itself. But to the extent that the body itself thus gives *itself* the impulse to vibrate, vocality can be considered, no longer the product of an external shock, but a sort of *percussion of the self.*[3]

With the exception of a fleeting allusion to the "singing voice of man" (addendum to §300 [139]), in the *Philosophy of Nature* Hegel only deals with animal voices. Most of these animal voices issue from an impulse or strike that is endured passively, that the individual *suffers*. Hegel thus writes, in the addendum to §358, that "every animal suffering violent death has a voice" by which it "declares its own supersession" (384); or, again in the addendum to §351:

> Birds of the air and other creatures emit cries when they feel pain, need, hunger, repletion, pleasure, joyfulness, or are in heat: the horse neighs when it goes to battle; insects hum; cats purr when pleased. (354)

Even if the vocal animal's bark, roar, or howl is thus already a sort of self-punctuation, its phonic manifestations are still induced by the implacable necessity of its survival or death. Only those of the bird testify, for Hegel, to a free expression, since, in contrast to the others, the bird's voice is not a "mere declaration of a need" (*bloßes Kundtun des Bedürfnisses*); it is no longer a "mere cry" (*bloßer Schrei*): It becomes "song" (*Gesang*), that is, the "immediate enjoyment of self" (*unmittelbare Genuss seiner selbst*) (409). In short, it is in this auto-affective vocality that externalizes the mere "feeling of self" (*Selbstgefühl*) that what Hegel calls the tendency to art or the artistic drive (*Kunsttrieb*) arises (addendum to §365 [409]).

The *Philosophy of Nature* thus anticipates the *Lectures on Fine Art*, which, symmetrically, carry out a sort of recapitulation of the *Philosophy of Nature.*[4]

But, beyond these crossings and cross-references, what await us now in Hegel's discourse on art and the arts are once again the remarkable entrances
of the point, which are inscribed in the series of dotted lines of all the ap-
pearances of punctiformity whose flickerings or leaps we have observed to
this point. And these points, which generally intervene at the major inflec-
tions of Hegel's discourse, which mark its grand logical articulations, thus
form a pulsating punctuation that is none other, we will see, than one of the
figures of the dialectic itself: The points of passage and halts in Hegel's narrative are connected by the pulsating rhythm of their systoles and diastoles,
in what one might describe as a sequence of *discontractions*.[5]

In the first paragraph of the third chapter, which takes up "artistic
beauty," Hegel thus writes:

> If we ask in which particular organ the whole soul appears as soul
> [*die ganze Seele als Seele erscheint*], we will at once name the eye; for
> in the eye the soul is concentrated [*in dem Auge konzentriert sich die
> Seele*], and the soul does not merely see through it [*und sieht nicht
> nur durch dasselbe*] but is also seen in it [*sondern wird auch darin
> gesehen*]. Now as the pulsating heart [*das pulsierende Herz*] shows
> itself all over the surface of the human, in contrast to the animal,
> body, so in the same sense is it to be asserted of art that it has to
> convert every shape in all points of its visible surface into an eye [*dass
> sie jede Gestalt an allen Punkten der sichtbare Oberfläche zum Auge
> verwandle*], which is the seat of the soul and brings the spirit into
> appearance. . . . Art makes every one of its productions [*Gebilde*] into
> a thousand-eyed Argus [*einem tausendäugigen Argus*], whereby the
> inner soul and spirit is seen at every point [*an allen Punkten*].[6]

The soul, here, is concentrated in the organ of vision, in the punctiform
eye, where it is at once seeing and seen. But this stigmatic contraction
precedes a dilation or dispersion that immediately multiplies the eye-
point into a cloud of points, transforming the entire surface of artistic
form into a sort of immense panoptic dotted line.

The lines we just read, let us recall, open the chapter on "artistic beauty"
(*das Kunstschöne*). Just before this, toward the end of the second chapter,
on "natural beauty" (*das Naturschöne*), Hegel seems already to set up the
analogy between, on the one hand, the heartbeat that shows in the blush-
ing of the surface of the skin and, on the other, the ocular animation of
the surface of the work of art. He writes:

> In [the human body] there is everywhere and always represented the
> fact that man is an ensouled and feeling unit [*ein beseeltes, empfin-*

dendes Eins ist]. The skin is not hidden by plant-like unliving coverings [*mit pflanzenhaft unlebendigen Hüllen verdeckt*]; the pulsation of the blood shows itself over the entire surface [*das Pulsieren des Blutes scheint an der ganzen Oberfläche*]; the beating heart of life is as it were present everywhere over the body [*das klopfende Herz der Lebendigkeit ist gleichsam allgegenwärtig*]. (146)

Once again, the *punctum saliens* of physiology is not far. It is there, visible between the lines, even if it is not named explicitly. Still more obviously than in the *Philosophy of Nature*, it here marks the dialectical passage from one moment to another: With its discontraction it punctuates the leap, the sublation, of natural beauty in artistic beauty.

But we also find this sublating punctuation again, for example, in the punctuated passages with which Hegel links the three Romantic arts: painting, music, and then poetry. And what plays out again in each of these passages is a sort of repetition of the beginning of the *Philosophy of Nature*, where the point found its punctuating efficacy by changing from space into time. Thus, in the introduction to the *Lectures on Fine Art*, Hegel says of painting that it "accept[s]" space, that is, the "indifferent self-externality" (*das gleichgültige Auseinander*) that was at issue in natural "Mechanics" (88): Painting "simulat[es]" the appearance of spatiality as self-externality, while music, to the contrary, "sublates" (*aufhebt*) it, "idealizes" (*idealisiert*) it, in "the individual singularity of the point" (*in das individuelle Eins des Punktes*) (88). And it is precisely in this that music constitutes the "middle point" (*Mittelpunkt*) (88) of the Romantic arts; it forms a "point of transition" (*Duchgangspunkt*) between painting and poetry (88).

Just as the point thus punctuates the transition from painting to music with its contracting diastole and systole, so too does it mark and inflect the sublation of music by poetry:

Sound in this way becomes a *word* as a voice [*Laute*] inherently articulated, the meaning of which is to articulate ideas and thoughts. The inherently negative point [*der in sich negative Punkt*] to which music had moved forward now comes forth as the completely concrete point, as the point of the spirit [*als der vollendet konkrete Punkt, als Punkt des Geistes*], as the self-conscious individual who out of his own resources unites the infinite *space* of his ideas with the *time* of sound. (88–89)

Such is the punctuation that divides Hegel's text on the Romantic arts into a discourse on painting, music, and poetry. Or better: Such is its *overpunctuation*, since the point is not content to emerge at the moment of the sublating passage from the one to the other; it does not merely mark or articulate sublation by accompanying or inflecting it—*it is also the very thing at stake in sublation.*

Here as elsewhere, in these pages from the *Lectures on Fine Art* as in so many other pages from the *Philosophy of Nature*, the point in fact overpunctuates the dialectical unfolding since it in a sense participates in it doubly • • twice at the same time:

• On the one hand, the point plays the role of link; it is an active character, so to speak, in the story of the logical deduction or reasoned engendering of one moment from the preceding one: As relay point, it constantly lends itself to the discontraction that ensures sublation.

• On the other hand, the point appears as the punctuation of this same story: It intervenes, we have seen, in spots in the narrative where it rubrics, paragraphs, and sections, where one leaps from one section to another (for example, from space to time, that is, from *a* to *b* at the beginning of the "Mechanics"), where one ascends from one title to the following one (for example, from "geological nature" to "organic nature," where life emerges, that is, from A to B in the "Organics"), where one transitions from chapter to chapter (for example, from the second to the third at the beginning of the *Lectures on Fine Art*, when "natural beauty" gives way to "artistic beauty" and its surface covered with punctiform eyes).

In short, the point is at once *in the story*—it is part of the *cast*, it is in the credits, so to speak—and *outside the story*—since it dictates its phrasing, gives it rhythm as that *distinctio* that it is (ₐ, • or •). The point, in a word, is at once an intra- and a metadiegetic instance.

On this double scene of overpunctuation what we might call the *point of an overcast stitch* [*point de surjet*] is weaved. Not only in the sense that this term has in sewing or surgery (for after all, in Hegel's *text*, it is a question of linking and articulation, of the knotting of moments into a woven *texture*).[7] But also in the sense that evokes an ascending movement made of *leaps toward the absolute.*

The leap is what one remarkable reading of Hegel, to which the preceding pages owe a great deal, literally names *Übersprung* in German.[8] It is what is produced, for example, when Hegel, in the passage of the *Lectures on Fine Art* above, speaks of the birth of musical sound as an idealizing absorption of the spatial exteriority of painting into "the individual singularity of the point" (*in das individuelle Eins des Punktes*).

Markus Semm then describes the sound that rings out as "the leap of a point [*das Überspringen eines Punktes*] that moves from the material to the spiritual" (145).

To leap would thus be, in this or that context, one possible synonym for the very movement of sublation, of internalizing *Aufhebung*, if it is understood without the machinic comfort that those who do not undergo the trial of *reading* Hegel, those content to postulate his driving principle, believe they can attribute to it. When there is leaping in Hegel's *text*, it is in fact never won, never given, in advance, as though it were but one more pulsation in the well-oiled mechanism of a heart whose beating irrigates the system.[9]

But if the leap is precisely merely another name for dialectical passage itself (perhaps we should say, instead, for clearing a path, to do justice to the effort, the resistance, that this passage meets), its movement remains strictly *internal* to the Hegelian system. It is merely another way of describing the hurdles or halts in the movement of this system—nicknames that at best would better emphasize the discontinuous and risky character of each step in this movement.

As for stigmatology, it cannot content itself with this. When it listens to *overpunctuation* in Hegel, it auscultates points of suture or overcast stitches of the text as places where its punctuation is at once intra- and metadiegetic, *and* as what takes place with or by the point in its circulation within the system, *and* as what makes possible its phrasing.

Why this attention to the doubling of the point? And what does phrasing mean in this case?

Gérard Genette has suggested that "every narrative" is a development—one that is as immense, "as monstrous as one might wish"[10]—of a minimal phrase (*À la recherche du temps perdu* being thus the extraordinary amplification of the syntagm "Marcel becomes a writer"). In the same way, to follow Markus Semm, we could read a whole part of Hegel's work as the unfolding that moves from the indifference between external points at the beginning of the *Philosophy of Nature* to the "point of the spirit" that the *Lectures on Fine Art* call to mind in speaking of the sublation of music by poetry. Thus, if the points that the dialectical phrase describes or mentions and the points that phrase this phrase are in a sense united, if the punctuated and punctuating points *cohere* in a certain manner, if there is, then, in their overpunctuating doubling some buttoning (as Lacan would say), well, when we touch on one, we also appeal to the other. In other words, to change the values—the rests (.), the breaths (•), the pauses (˙)—of punctuating punctuation, that is, to change the inflection of the narration, is to open the possibility of shaking the *narrative*. It is in any case to give oneself the chance for this—without any assurance as to the import of the shock that such a shaking will imprint on the narrative edifice. If this narrative edifice resists—in fact, it is rare that it gives way—it is no doubt because we will have recited it with a phrasing that, while it seems new, in reality only places the emphasis where it was expected.[11]

In an addendum to one of the first paragraphs from his introduction to the *Philosophy of Nature*, Hegel cited these words by Johann Georg Hamann, taken from a letter to Kant dated December 1759:

> "Nature," Hamann therefore rightly says, "is a Hebrew word written only with consonants [*das mit blossen Mitlautern geschrieben wird*] and the understanding must point it [*zu dem der Verstand die Punkte setzen muss*]." (§ 246 [109])

Which is to say that we must appose to this word vowels, which the Hebrew alphabet does not note but which the points supplement. But if nature or the real thus awaits vowel sonorities that will make them a *voiced* discourse, this discourse in turn lends itself to all the punctuations and overpunctuations whose beats we have auscultated.

.

"The point represented above, exactly at the instant that it is perceived, begins to expand in every direction towards infinity: it continues to expand, at the speed of light, for the entire time that these words are being read, but returns to its original essence instantly after the last word has been read."

With this work, fascinating in its obviousness and meant to be seen and read at the same time,[1] the American conceptual artist Douglas Huebler (1924–1997) was able to capture or encapsulate what we might call *the phrasing of the point*, understanding the expression in terms of both values of the genitive, the subjective and the objective. The phrasing *of* the point, yes, in the double sense that it is, on the one hand, the point that *is phrased*—the point, as it appears in the middle of the page, is unfolded further down in a sentence [*période*] that describes its dilation and contraction; and, on the other hand, the point that *phrases*—for what else marks the last word with a final period [*point final*] in which it again coincides with itself? In short, the point represented • is the object, the theme, of the sentence that relates its diastole and systole. But this sentence is in turn inflected by the repetition of the same point • that triggered and now punctuates it, closing it off• The point is thus also the actor, the subject, of this sentence.

Phrased and phrasing, alternately dilated and contracted, *discontracted*, the point is caught exemplarily in that movement that I have tried to describe as overpunctuation. And its pulsating mechanism here appears suffused with clarity that even the most didactic discourse would struggle to achieve. But Douglas Huebler's work also evokes still another aspect of phrasing or punctuation, another dimension of punctuating force, to which stigmatology must pay close attention: ekphrasis.

Ekphrasis is often defined as the verbal—literary—description of a painting or image. And if we provisionally stick to this classic definition,[2] the point unfolded then refolded by Huebler is in fact the limit case of ekphrasis, a sort of linguistic stretching or expansion of the point by the point. The question that emerges in this phrased self-pointing—and it of course calls to mind the pointing out that points itself out at the beginning of Hegel's *Phenomenology of Spirit*—the question, from here on, is this: What about punctuation and the image, the punctuation of the image?

To approach this question, I take a long detour, follow what will seem like a Tristramesque digression that in reality will lead to the heart of what is at stake in ekphrasis: the overpunctuation of the image and, perhaps, the image itself *as* overpunctuated pulsation.

Let's get going, then, take a detour, a fork in the road that is not one.

In Kafka's unfinished novel *The Trial* there is a passage that has always given me a kind of vertigo. To my mind, these are its most discretely terrifying pages before the famous and overwhelming parable "Before the Law," the only fragment published in the author's lifetime. They are found in the chapter titled "The Lawyer, The Factory Owner, The Painter."[3]

K. is starting to think his lawyer is doing nothing for him and that he himself will have to present to the court a "submission" (*Eingabe*), a sort of memoir that he has to provide for his defense:

> Preparing the submission was an almost unending task. You didn't have to lack self-confidence to quickly come to feel it was impossible ever to complete the submission . . . because, ignorant as he was of the charges against him, not to mention any possible extension of them, he would have to pass his whole life in review and describe it right down to the very last detail. (91)

A bit like in the impossible undertaking of the autobiotristramography, Joseph K. knows that he will never coincide with himself, with an exact image or narrative of himself, through the memoir containing his memories.

Later in the same chapter, this impossible and yet alarming totalization of the self is no longer inflected in the register of speech or discourse (by composing a submission that is doomed to remain unfinished) but in the relationship between K. and the image. On the recommendation of one of his clients at the bank where he works, he visits a painter who goes by the pseudonym Titorelli and who works "for the court" (*für das Gericht*) (97). Titorelli, he believes, he is told, will be able to offer advice leading to his acquittal.

Not finding the artist's studio, K., under the pretext that he "want[s] him to paint [his portrait]" (*ich will mich von ihm malen lassen*) (101), asks one of the four girls he sees passing by if a painter by the name of Titorelli lives there. Then, when K. finally arrives at his studio, Titorelli says, "Have you come to buy paintings or to have yourself painted?" (*Wollen Sie Bilder kaufen oder sich selbst malen lassen?*) (103). Astonished, surprised by this question, which his letter of introduction should have allowed him to avoid, K. does not respond. Or, more precisely, he replies by asking in turn,

> "You're working on a painting at the moment [*an einem Bild*]?" "Yes," said the painter. . . . It's a portrait [*Porträt*]. A good piece of work, but not quite finished yet." (103)

Before the unfinished painting, the dialogue that follows between K. and the painter is thus placed under the sign of ambiguity or of something unsaid. K. has come to ask for advice on how to conduct his trial. And yet he doesn't wish to appear impolite by dismissing the possibility of having his portrait done. He even appears interested in the canvas on the easel, which, he learns, depicts a judge seated on a throne adorned with an allegorical figure, half Justice, half Victory.

The potential solution for K.'s impossible submission is thus deferred by an image. Or, more precisely, by the description of an image in the process of being made, since K. briefly observes the painter painting:

> [Titorelli] rolled up his sleeves, took several crayons, and K. looked
> on as [*sah zu, wie*], round the head of the judge, the quivering points
> of the crayons [*unter den zitternden Spitzen der Stifte*] created [*sich
> bildete*] a reddish shadow like a sunburst, which faded away towards
> the edge of the picture [*gegen den Rand des Bildes*]. Gradually the
> shadow encircled the head, like an adornment or a sign of distinction.
> Around the figure of Justice, however, it remained bright, apart from
> some imperceptible shading, and in the brightness the figure seemed
> to advance more than ever, it hardly recalled the Goddess of Justice
> any more, nor the Goddess of Victory either, rather, it looked com-
> pletely like the Goddess of the Hunt. (105)

These lines look a lot like the old rhetorical figure of ekphrasis, which, so far as I am aware, is rare in Kafka.[4] It is in fact the process [*processus*] of this canvas in progress, of which the narrative in a sense gives an account [*procès-verbal*], that here defers the potential resolution of K.'s improb-able trial [*procès*]. While the painting [*Bild*] is taking shape [*sich bildet*], the outcome of the trial, happy or unhappy, still awaits. As though the one were substituted for the other.

K.'s dialogue with the painter proceeds under the voyeuristic gaze of the girls who pointed the studio out to him and who now spy on him from behind the door: "They were probably crowding round the key-hole, perhaps it was possible to see in through the gaps in the door" (105). Nothing in the scene escapes these girls who await the moment when K., they believe, will pose for Titorelli.

Finally, Titorelli seems to resign himself to helping K., to considering solutions with him. He asks him, "Are you innocent?" (106). Of course, K. responds; but, he immediately continues, this innocence hardly simplifies matters:

> "When the court does bring charges it is firmly convinced of the
> guilt of the accused and can only be persuaded to change its mind
> with difficulty." "With difficulty?" the painter asked, throwing up one

hand. "The court can never be persuaded to change its mind. If I were to paint all the judges on a canvas here and you defended yourself before the canvas [*vor dieser Leinwand verteidigen*], you'd have more chance of success than before the real court [*vor dem wirklichen Gericht*]." (107)

Before the canvas, then, as before the court: It is as though, more and more, pictorial frame and judiciary space come to be superposed upon, or substituted for, each other even in the infinite deferral that postpones or delays their closure. For it is indeed a question of an incessant adjournment, of a deadline constantly pushed back, in short, of a *différance* of the image as of the verdict—and even of the verdict or veridiction *of the image as such*.

K. soon learns with dismay that no one can remember the court ever granting an acquittal. Or, more precisely, no "genuine acquittal" (*wirklichen Freispruch*) (110). Two other possibilities remain, then, which the painter names "apparent [*scheinbar*] acquittal" and "protraction of the proceedings" (*Verschleppung*) (110). In reality they amount to the same thing, since, as Titorelli will say, "the second acquittal is followed by the third arrest, the third acquittal by the fourth arrest, and so on" (114). Facing an increasingly discouraged K., he will conclude, in short, that the absence of an end point is "all part of the concept of apparent acquittal" (114).

There is therefore no other prospect, the painter explains, than endless procrastination. His account of the two possible solutions—both of which amount to stalling—is delayed again not only by the "dizziness" (*Schwindel*) (111) that overcomes K. in the heat of the studio, but especially, once he has taken off his jacket, by the girls who once again crowd "round the gaps to see the spectacle for themselves" (111–12).

> "You see, the girls all think I'm going to paint you [*dass ich Sie malen werde*]," the painter said, "and that you're getting undressed for it." "Do they now," said K., only mildly amused, for he didn't feel any better despite the fact that he was in his shirtsleeves. It was almost in a grumpy voice that he asked, "What did you call the two other possibilities?"—he'd already forgotten the terms. "Apparent acquittal and protraction of the proceedings," said the painter. (112)

It would almost seem that postponement itself never comes to an end. Like the Tristramesque interinterruptions, it *postpones itself* before the canvas, before this construction site of the image that is deferred in being formed.

In his 1962 film based on Kafka's *The Trial*, Orson Welles emphasizes and further accentuates the superposition, this sort of narrative overwriting,[5] of the interminable trial and postponed portrait. In the sequence corresponding to the pages we have just read, we see a close-up of the faces of the girls who appear between the slats in the door and the studio walls, then a low angle, medium close-up shot of the painter, with K. in the background:

TITORELLI. They seem to think I'm going to paint your portrait, and that's why you've taken off your jacket.

K. What are the . . . other alternatives? (*High angle reverse shot.*)

TITORELLI. Um . . . You mean the legal alternatives?

K. Yes.

TITORELLI. (*Rather petulantly*). I told you! Ostensible acquittal or indefinite deferment.[6]

At the precise instant when the shot reverses to a high angle, there is a moment of wavering in the dialogue: perhaps for the painter to consider alternatives to painting K.'s portrait? This doubt indeed seems to take hold of Titorelli for a second when he hesitates ("um . . .") then thinks he is obligated to remove the ambiguity with his question ("you mean the legal alternatives").

This brief point of indetermination, marked by the change in camera angle, allows us to understand that, even more than in the novel, one must phrase *vor der Leinwand*, before the canvas, to defer judgment. One must chatter to space the image and stall the verdict; one must banter [*bonimenter*][7] to put off symbolically the crystallization of the icon of the imaginary law. *Before the image, then, as before the law*: This is what a number of sequences in Welles's film will make visible. But before coming to them, and so as to get a good sense of what is at stake, we must take the time to go briefly through the ancient history of ekphrasis again. Which is the prelude, from afar, to that of the film explainer [*bonimenteur*].

Ekphrasis is that ancient rhetorical figure that Homer exemplified with his description of Achilles' shield at the end of the eighteenth book of the *Iliad*. It is a way of making phrases (of expressing or explaining: *phrazein*) that translates and exhausts a visual representation in language (the prefix *ek* here indicates completion rather than a movement to the outside).[8] It is a phrasing of images or paintings, a discourse that seeks to be exhausting or exhaustive as it conveys an object—at first perceived as self-contained—into the externality of a chain of words.

One of the most beautiful ancient ekphrases that I have had occasion to read is by Ovid in the sixth book of the *Metamorphoses*. Here, briefly, is its context.

Arachne is an artist of the loom. She weaves; she works with wool like no other. Her talent is such that the nymphs come to contemplate her admirable work (*opus admirabile*). And, Ovid insists (line 15), it gives them pleasure to look at not only the completed cloths (*nec factas solum vestes spectare*) but those being made (*tum quoque cum fierent*). Not only the work, then, but—and perhaps most of all—the process.

Arachne, however, denies that she owes her gift to Minerva, the goddess who presides over the arts and artisans. She even defies her: "Contend with me," she says (*certet mecum*, line 25). Soon, preparations are made for the competition (*certamina*): The looms are set up; the competitors weave (*texitur*); and in the cloths are spun ancient stories (*vetus in tela deducitur argumentum*, line 69). Arguments or narratives are woven, threaded, into the texture of the cloth. And it is here that Ovid enters into a detailed description of the tapestries—first Minerva's (lines 70–102) and then Arachne's (lines 103–28)—which represent scenes of gods and goddesses. In short, ekphrasis begins the moment the threads of the textile and the textual intermingle in a contexture that complicates the one with the other, that co-implicates weaving and the tessitura of the narrative voice. Ultimately, the competitors also interweave the linguistic textures of the Latin *texere*, *textura*, *textus*, *textum*, and the rest, *et cetera*.

I will pass over the development of the ekphrases themselves, the long, *extended* descriptions,[9] to get to the end, to what is tied together [*se noue*] in the dénouement (127–45).

Giving her cloth a final touch, Arachne surrounds it with a narrow border in which flowers are interwoven with entangled ivy, *intertextos*. Interweaving, *intertexere*: This is Arachne's final gesture. And it is also the final word, the ultimate signifier that marks the stopping point of the ekphrasis, that signs its conclusion at line 128.

For the image in the cloth lasted only as long as its intertexture with the text that phrases it: Once completed, barely knotted, or stabilized in its inextricably iconic and verbal contexture, it is interrupted by Minerva's angry tearing of it (*rupit*). We know what comes next: Arachne, beside herself with rage, ties a knot around her throat (*laqueoque animosa ligavit guttura*) and hangs herself; but, moved to pity, Minerva allows her to survive, while at the same time punishing her with her metamorphosis into a spider. From then on, Arachne produces thread (*remittit stamen*) and busies herself (*exercet*) with her ancient cloths (*antiquas telas*). There she is, then, the weaver stripped of speech (or at least of ears, *aures*, with which to hear it, since she loses them in changing form in line 141); there she is, untied from the lace (*laqueus*) with which she wanted to kill herself only to find herself tied again to the task of weaving cloths that, one imagines, *no longer mean anything*.

Ovid's arachnean ekphrasis, if one reads it as we just have, is thus essentially an *intertext*. It does not take the place of the image; it consists and makes the image consist in interlacing itself with it, like ivy that holds up the tree that supports it.[10] This is what I believe distinguishes Ovid's version of this rhetorical figure from the classical examples of pictorial description that come before and after him. Thus, at the very beginning of the first book of *Daphnis and Chloe* (a pastoral attributed to Longus, a Greek author believed to have lived in the second century CE), the narrator, hunting in woods on the island of Lesbos, stops short before "a painted image, a love story" (*eikona graptēn, historian erōtos*). A strange encounter, this, with an image right in the middle of the forest. And which paints a picture still more charming than that of the surrounding nature:

> Fair also [*kalon men kai*] was the grove, thick with trees, flowery, well watered: a single spring nourished it all, flowers and trees alike. But that depiction was lovelier still [*all'hē graphē terpnotera*], owning outstanding technique [*technēn*]. . . . Its prestige drew many visitors, even strangers, . . . to view the image [*eikonos theatai*]. In it were women giving birth and other women adorning babies in swaddling clothes, babies abandoned and breasts feeding them. . . . I looked and marveled [*thaumasanta*], and a longing [*pothos*] seized me to rival the depiction in words [*antigrapsai tēi graphēi*]; I sought an interpreter of the image [*exēgētēn tēs eikonos*] and have carefully fashioned four books.[11]

Barbara Cassin quite rightly comments that this passage is "responding" with a written story to a painting that is itself already a story, a *histo-*

ria. It responds in writing (*antigraphein*), *countergraphing*, we might say, the graphic image of drawing or painting (*graphē*). For my part, I also hear the paradigm of the copy (*antigraphon*) resonate in the Greek verb, that is, not only the response *to* but the replica *of* the image. Whether response or mimetic transcription, it remains the case that ekphrasis comes to take over for painting here; it is written instead, and in the place, of the image (*anti*); it is exchanged with, *against*, it. And it seems, moreover, to presuppose that mysterious intermediary that is the exegete (*exēgētēn*): Longus does not compose pastorals directly from images but rather by following an interpretation that is already interposed between writing and the painting.[12]

In short, whether description or description of description, the narrative writing of Longus's story comes after the fact, after the image, substituting itself for it and confirming it by reproducing it. In Ovid, by contrast, one might say that the narrative is *entirely against* the image, with both the icon and the phrase consisting only of that intertexture that, for lack of a better term, I call an *iconophrase* in order to mark that it is the verbal or vocal tessitura that weaves the image while deferring the moment of its capture or crystallization.

But why recall these moments in the very old—and yet so new—history of ekphrasis?

Because ekphrasis is not only a description, as its classical definition would have it, but, more precisely, a *de-scription*, with the hyphen's typographic gap as the mark of union or disunion, which Philippe Lacoue-Labarthe suggested in a posthumous essay.[13] To be sure, ekphrastic writing would thus produce a translation of the image into the symbolic order of logos, and words or narrative voice, accordingly, refer to the icon that is their source. But even in *positing* it thus as their origin, they *depose* it; they uninscribe it; they remove it from its established verticality, displacing it into the chatter of language. In short, if one wished to distinguish two forces—which in reality compose one another—in the rhetoric of ekphrasis, one could say that Longus's magnifies the image as an original monument, whereas Ovid's stretches it as far as the eye can see in the intertext of language in which it at once consists and desists.

Still more than Kafka's, Welles's *The Trial* is continually shaped by the fear of the freeze frame [*arrêt sur image*] (an expression that we would almost have to understand in terms of a court decree or judgment, as an *arrest*

on or of the image), as though it were a matter of adjourning its fixation, its hold, and its grasp. As long as K. and Titorelli are *talking* about the portrait (which we do not see), we are almost reassured. We know that the trial [*procès*], the process, will continue, that there is no definitive verdict yet. And we have an inkling, we get the feeling, that if the voices go quiet in the face of the image, it will freeze into a magnified gaze: that gaze, as Lacan said, that is "outside," that is on the "side of things," that gaze by which "I am looked at," "I am photo-graphed," that gaze "which turns me into a picture."[1]

Already when K. and Titorelli are before the canvas, commenting on it, when they make and unmake it by interweaving words, when they *intertext* it, the girls' eyes, in a close-up between the boards, recall in re-

turn or *from behind*, as it were, the *watching* power of the image hidden from us.

A little later K. and the painter sit down on the bed. K. is discouraged: "No use trying either, I suppose," he says, while Titorelli confirms that there is, in fact, "not a hope."[2] And their dialogue is more than ever punctuated by the looks that multiply around them. Behind the boards framing the studio in which K. seems to renounce all possibility of loosening the imaginary noose that captures him, the proliferation of eyes appears to form a sort of hyper-vigilant Argus, like the panoptic surface of the work of art as Hegel describes it.

This is why K. has to flee this image, which he cannot undo and which constantly re-forms, encircling him with its gazes. The long sequence

of his flight through a hallway made of openwork boards, then through underground tunnels and galleries pierced with eye-holes, through which the girls continue to stare at him, this chase is K.'s desperate attempt to escape being captured by and in the image. What he attempts to elude by taking to his heels, we have already read in the novel, is the hold or grasp, the verdict or veridiction, of this canvas, of this painting before which he finds himself as though before the court—*vor der Leinwand als vor dem Gericht*.

But the German *Leinwand* also names a cinema screen—in French, moreover, one says, "se faire une toile," "to go to a movie" [literally, "to make a canvas"—Trans.]—that screen on which are projected the films Kafka, we know, was so fond of.[3] It is thus also before the screen that K. again finds himself as though before the law. And before a screen that, at the time Kafka went to the cinema, was silent. Or rather, since this supposed mutism is largely a retrospective fiction, at a time when the projection was systematically talked through, explained, narrated, *lectured*, as it

were: Beside the screen of the law of the image stood this strange character, *the film explainer*, of whom there are so many echoes in Welles's film.

This is why, after my brief traversal of the history of ekphrasis, I now
take the time to recall that of the cinema narrator—*der Kinoerzähler*, as
he is called in German. Like K., like all of us, he too carries out what
Philippe Lacoue-Labarthe called the de-scription of the image, so that it
doesn't hold us in its grasp—not too much, not completely.

He too phrases the image; he too—we will come to this—overpunctuates it and makes it pulsate, leap.

In a remarkable volume on film explaining, Germain Lacasse reminds
us that the ancestor of this speaker or phraser, who goes by various names
(*lecturer* in English, *benshi* in Japanese, *filmuitlegger* in Dutch, *explicador*
in Spanish), is the "one who shows the magic lantern." Called *fatiste* or
factiste, there is evidence of him going back to sixteenth-century Paris.[4]
Later, he will also be referred to as "lanternist," like a certain Étienne-
Gaspard Robertson, who at the time of the Revolution projected images
onto smoke by means of a "fantascope" and also employed a ventriloquist
named Fritz-James (51). He is also described as "conférencier" (conference speaker), "bonimenteur" (film explainer), or "bonisseur" (story-
teller), but also as *termagi* in Brittany (a contraction of the words *lanterne*
and *magique*), as "montreur de villes" (city guide) in Quebec, and so on.

In a beautiful autobiographical narrative devoted to his film explainer
grandfather, the German writer Gert Hofmann repeatedly emphasizes that
the origin of his grandfather's strange profession is in the fairground:

> In his youth, Grandfather had once worked in the circus. . . . In that
> circus Grandfather had appeared in a uniform, first to announce the
> individual acts. Later on he led the artists into the arena by the hand,
> and introduced them to the public. . . . When he announced the acts,
> he stood between the director and the clown. . . . Grandfather took
> so much pleasure from it that instead of sticking to the task [*statt bei
> der Sache zu bleiben*], he sometimes tried to add [*dazuzudichten*] little
> stories [*kleine Geschichten*]. . . . In the process, he made the show un-
> necessarily long, and had to be replaced.[5]

A kind of phraser of everything, the protagonist doesn't exactly have
a profession or art: "Grandfather is an artist," the narrator's mother declares; "he just needs to discover in what field" (34). And in the same way,
those who live in Limbach, the small Saxon community where he serves
as explainer of the films shown at the Apollo cinema, don't know how to

"place" this man who "had already had so many jobs [*Berufe*], and not a proper one among them" (38).

If he appears unclassifiable, it is because, coming from street theater or variety shows, from fairs or the circus, the film explainer displaces the silent filmic image from its proper field. He makes it improper, impure, precisely in order to make it "good": good for sales, to be sure, but also a good distraction, good to take in, good to tell.[6] He makes it popular; he deposes the fascinating authority of the spectral images that float without mooring by integrating them into a speech that is intentionally local, a dialect (thus his grandfather speaks a "Saxon dialect" [53]). In short, as Germain Lacasse puts it quite rightly, the practice of the film explainer is a "practice of appropriation"; his power lies in his "ability to make a text his own and to reorganize it according to all the conventions familiar to a specific audience" (*Le Bonimenteur de vies animées*, 124–25).

By tearing the image from the iconic field proper to it, by making it improper, the film explainer can appropriate it, that is, make it good, proper, *for* something, even if this means making it lie by improving it. In this, his artless art, his professionless profession, is like that of musical arrangers or adaptors, to whom I have devoted a number of pages elsewhere. Or like that of the *claqueurs* who have also long captivated me; in the nineteenth century, they gave rhythm to, marked, and articulated concerts with their applause, producing a sort of convincing auditory phrasing of the concerts, imposing on the audience a clapped punctuation.[7]

The art of the film explainer seems to have had its peak in cinema with the figure of the *benshi* in Japan, as Lacasse demonstrates: The performance of certain film explainers there was so prized that it could be "sold on disk"; there were also *benshi* "competitions," "tournaments" of sorts, during which the film explainers "commented on the same film" one after the other (134).

Now, this competitive or warring dimension of film explaining, as was also the case for the auditory *claque*, is aimed at the audience at the same time that it applies to the work. "Scanning the screen and the hall alternately," the *benshi* is that "intermediary" who "in practice orchestrates a dialogue between the film and the audience" (135), just as at the concert the leader of the *claque* determined the beginning, length, and intensity of the applause and was thus transformed into a sort of conductor, the mirror or double of the other, directing the audience as the conductor does the musicians.

This is why, moreover, like the *claqueur*'s listening, the film explainer's watching is partial in every sense of the word, doubled as he is between observing the film and the spectators he would like to lead, to direct through the images. Grandfather Hofmann, who is said to have "poor eyesight," thus confides:

> When I was really excited by a scene [*wenn mich eine Stelle packte*], I stood up on my box-seat—an old tea chest from Ceylon—and stared at the audience [*und habe ins Publikum geschaut*]. . . . Severely [*streng*]. (*Film Explainer*, 5)

After experiencing its golden age at the turn of the twentieth century, film explaining nevertheless disappeared as cinema was institutionalized, a process Lacasse describes precisely: Preparing the ground for film to be adopted as art, film explaining, before it passed away, became a practice of local, and even "anticolonial," resistance against an institution seen as "universal."[8] However strong and necessary this so to speak geopolitical analysis of film explaining, it nonetheless does not exclude a different perspective: that film explanation—like adaptation, the *claque*, and the other practices I have grouped under the generic term *derangement*—in the end had to yield before a *structural*, that is, *internal*, perception of the *work*. The end of film explanation, from this point of view, would correspond to its internalizing integration into the filmic work that is organically closed upon itself, become structure.[9] And the filmic work, as such, will gradually undertake its own narrative explication, offer its own lecture on itself. The vocal instance or responsibility for explanation thus gradually moves *into the film*. And we still hear the distant remains of this process, the echoes or traces of this internalization, when Godard *speaks* the credits at the beginning of *Mépris*, as Welles does at the end of *The Trial*, after the explosion that puts the final period on the narrative.[10] We might even say that Welles, when he coun-tersigns his film out loud, after having listed the actors ("I wrote and directed this film. My name is Orson Welles" [176], he says), puts precisely what had resisted the authorial affirmation of the work, that is, film explaining, at

its service. And the very last image, that of the door of the law that closes, is not far from calling to mind, instead and in the place of the traditional words "The End," a symbol for the closure of the filmic image on itself, on the autonomy of *its* law.

But just as the otographic practice of the *claque* does not take place only on the public scene of the concert, so too ekphrastic film explanation occurs and continues to unfold in the absence of projection in a theater, that is, on that internal screen that grandfather Hofmann calls to mind: "Every human being . . . carries a cinema screen in his head [*jeder Mensch trägt . . . ein Kino in seinem Kopf*]," he declares to his slightly surprised grandson, before adding, "and the name of that screen is . . . imagination [*Phantasie*]!" (156). This is why, moreover, "before telling the film to other people, Grandfather had to tell it to himself first [*erst sich selbst erzählen musste*]" (8). There is thus an explanation before the explanation, an arche-explainer, as it were, in each of us as we look at the image, weaving or interweaving it—*intertexting* it, Ovid would say—with words and gestures. Accordingly, the conflict between the authoritative self-commentary of the work and the explanatory punctuation of the long-winded lecturer, embodied in the bitter debate between the owner of the Apollo in Limbach and his employee Karl Hofmann, is far from being limited strictly to the history of cinematographic institutions. The tragicomic dispute in the novel, when one asks "whether your incessant chattering doesn't actually irritate the public" (for, he argues "after all, there are subtitles"), and the other responds, "No, . . . it's not superfluous" (50), also plays out internally in the intimacy of every gaze.

The figure of the film explainer indeed ends up disappearing from the visible scene of the history of cinema—and it is essentially its mourning that Hofmann's novel narrates. A mourning that already begins during the grandfather's lifetime, when he drags his grandson along on "tours of inspection" (42) around Limbach, during which they notice that "in none of the cinemas was there a film explainer" (47). But this impossible and interminable mourning also takes place in the child's memory; after the fact, it divides *his memory of watching the film* when he falls asleep on the return trip from their expeditions in these neighboring counties where films are now shown without commentary:

> Then we'd watch the film, say we'd liked it, but we had to dash, otherwise we'd see the last bus—or train—just pulling away from under our noses. In the train—or bus—Grandfather would tell the film to me once more, the way *he* understood it. Often he had understood it quite differently

from me. I thought: Why does everyone understand every film differently? and, so thinking, fell asleep [*und schlief über der Frage ein*]. (48)

On this "blank screen of my sleepless nights" that a beautiful song by Claude Nougaro sings of,[11] on this screen where "I make movies," the grandson's question continues to resonate in us, in the midst of the ekphrases of film explainers that are interlaced with our gaze, allowing it to exist.

In this sense our eyesight is "bad," like that of Karl Hofmann, who "only sees what he wants to see" (*er sieht bloss, was er will*) (5): only what he wants to see with a gaze that, not without difficulty, sees by means of deictics that are the marks of his artless art. For what does the grandfather do if not point out by punctuating, for example, when he presents, among so many other silent films evoked in the novel and now forgotten, Robert Wiene's adaptation of Maurice Renard's fantasy novel, *Les Mains d'Orlac* (1924)? Let's watch the cinema narrator at work:

> *There* is Orlac lying on his belly [*da liegt Orlac auf dem Bauch*], and *here* he comes crawling [*da kommt er angekrochen*], cried Grandfather from his chest; note his wonderful pallor! The cause of which, he cried, is the accident he has just had. . . . In this car accident, Grandfather explained, the brilliant virtuoso pianist . . . loses both his hands. But a surgeon hurries along, and deftly replaces them with the hands of a freshly executed murderer, said Grandfather, and *pointed with this stick* [*und zeigt mit seinem Stöckchen*] at the old severed hands and the freshly attached new ones. And *there* [*und da*], the shadows of his old hands, and *here* [*und da*], of the new ones! (38–39, my emphasis)

Here, the film explainer never stops saying (and saying *to himself*): *Look at this*; look there (*da*, in German), as though he himself were a sort of pointing stick, that is, a deictic dedicated to pointing out. The film explainer punctuates by pointing, as though he were running desperately after the self-evidence of indexicality. He pulls out all the stops to mark, to phrase, the images passing by: Grandfather, the narrator says, also spoke "with his hands and feet" (*mit den Händen und den Füssen*) (38); he "stood up on tiptoe" (*stellte er sich auf die Zehenspitzen*) (41).[12] But in doing so, the film explainer also seems to point at himself *en abyme* as the instance of pointing;[13] he doubles and divides himself constantly by exhorting himself to punctuate, by dotting his own punctuation in an escalation—overpunctuating—that establishes him as the hyperbolic point of scopic pulsion:

He drove himself on and said [*er trieb sich selbst an und rief*]: On, on old man [*weiter, weiter, alter Mann*], forward, forward [*und voran, voran*]! And he would get up and rock on the balls of his feet [*Dabei stellte er sich auf die Zehnespitzen und wippte*]. (36)

More than a simple deictic, the film explainer is thus its doubling repetition, its immediate echo; he is that burst of showing that is marked in the German text of Hofmann's novel by the iteration of the *here* (*da*), accompanying and remarking the inherent ostension of the punctuating gaze:

Grandfather, with his bamboo stick, pointed at the screen [*Der Grossvater, mit dem Bambusstock, zeigte auf das Bild*]. That way the scene was there twice over. ["*Here* it was twice *here*," one would no doubt have to write to translate this untranslatable sentence: *Da war die Stelle denn zweimal da.*] (40)

In short, just as the *claque* is listening as marking, explaining in the broadest sense is simply the gaze as punctuation. It is the stigmatic life or pulsation of the gaze, its beat (its *punctum saliens*, Hegel might say), as the narrator describes it touchingly at the very end of the novel, remembering his dead grandfather's words:

Grandfather at seventy said: In the beginning was the light. The light was switched off. I stood in front of the screen, all alone. I looked into the audience. There weren't many of them there. I gave the signal *Go!* He said: In all the films of that time, even if they played indoors, it rained. That was because the films had been damaged by the fingers of the projectionists. We lined the gate with black velvet to show the film. Even that damaged it. Also, they got old and worn. Grandfather took me by the hand. He said: It wasn't the shaking projection that made everything tremble. Nor was it people's breathing. It was the heartbeat of the man who was supervising everything, the film explainer's, mine. (250)

Yes, *vor der Leinwand*: before the screen or canvas, as before the image, there is the leaping rhythm of a viewpoint—*punctum saliens videns*.

Orson Welles filmed the indoor sequences of *The Trial* in Paris (in the old Orsay train station) and the outdoor sequences in Zagreb. But the film opens and closes with a singular image that belongs nowhere, that was filmed neither here nor there, in Zagreb or Paris, but *on the screen itself.*

This image, which follows the opening credits and is also the final image after the closing ones, was in fact produced by a device called a pin screen. Without knowing what this device is, we might think of a disturbing machine that from afar calls to mind the one Kafka imagines in "In the Penal Colony." There it is a question of inscribing, of typographing with a terrifying punctuating acupuncture, the law, or more precisely the condemnation to death, with everything that follows from it, right on the body of the condemned, which is thus stigmatized. A condemnation that

thus coincides with its inscription, but will remain unreadable by the condemned himself, since he dies as it is inscribed on his skin.

The pin screen of *The Trial*, while it appears to have nothing to do with such a torture device, while it is simply one technique among others for producing images (it was invented by Alexandre Alexeieff and Claire Parker, who used it in animated films), nevertheless bears or incarnates something of the law of the image. For there is, here, inscribed right in the image (as on the surface of the screen or canvas, *auf der Leinwand*) what Jean-Luc Nancy has named its *distinction*.[14]

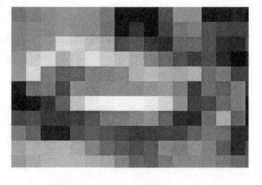

Not only in the sense of the image being distinguished, as image, from the thing it is supposed to represent, but also in the distinctness that it produces *in itself*; that is, it presents itself as already punctuated, marked, or inflected. In short, if the image is distinct (from the Latin *distinguere*, which comes from the Greek *diastizein*, which is formed from the distributive prefix *dia* and the radical *stig*, which, we recall, indicates a stitch or puncture), this is not only because it is separate as image but also and above all because it is *stigmatic* in its construction or texture. It always has *dots*; it can even be *grainy* (as one says of unclear photographs) or pixelated (as one says of a low resolution digital image). And if the opening image of *The Trial* is exemplary in this sense, it is because it is pricked with a pin or stigmatized *at every point*.[15]

Now, it is precisely this image that is *already punctuated through and through* that Welles's voice-over comments on, like a good old film explainer or lanternist. When he relates, at the beginning of the film and then more briefly at the end, the parable titled "Before the Law," his narrative, his ekphrastic explanation, is an overpunctuation of that punctuation that the internal definition of the image as distinct already is. It is a stigmatization added to it, but added in advance or from the beginning, if I can put it thus, for it is the weaving of the gaze itself.

It is in this way, always, that I appropriate for myself the image that looks at and dots me, overpunctuating it. Unless it's the other way around,

unless it's the image that, as I am striving to punctuate it by narrating it to myself in the course of my explaining gazes, surrounds and encircles me, attempts to take hold of me with the hypergaze of its salient points, as though it were chasing me, like the eyes of the girls chasing after K., in the infinite procession of the oculi that scan the hallway in which he flees before the image.

Who is taking stock of whom, between the image that looks at me and me looking at it? Who fixes the other? Who nails the other with a look? We no doubt find here what Jean-Luc Nancy would call a "distinct oscillation,"[16] a reciprocal stigmatization, though with no possible reciprocity, with no stable end or coincidence.

The end of Welles's *The Trial* seems to want to put a face to this terror, to the panic of gazes facing each other—me facing the image, the image facing me—to this mad vacillation of punctuation and overpunctuation. The law of the image that looks at me—that observes me from the "outside," that Lacan situated "on the side of things"—assumes a reassuring and human appearance, as menacing as it is: that of the lawyer. And so, the strange pin screen images from the prologue

become a simple background against which the silhouettes of the two voices now stand out.

Against the stigmatic background of these punctuated icons, concealing them as well, K. and his lawyer (Anthony Perkins and Orson Welles himself) confront each other. "What's this," K. demands, striking the table on which the projector sits, emphasizing thus that the coming scene will be at least as much a debate on the filmic image itself as on the legal destiny of the protagonist. And the lawyer responds, "We use these visual aids."[17] As though the images had been domesticated in the service of a discourse, as though they had become simple prostheses or illustrations of a rhetoric. Exasperated, K., moreover, exclaims, "Lectures and sermons!" (166). He all but treats the lawyer as a *lecturer*, a conference speaker, or a film explainer.

Thus, when we now again hear Welles's voice repeat the parable from the beginning before the same pin images, it has lost its spectral authority, it is almost nothing but the voice of a shady lawyer immediately contradicted by that of his client. For K. interrupts without hesitation, reducing the parable to a sort of cliché: "I've heard it all before. We've all heard it" (166). While the images of the doors of the law pass as they did at the beginning, their commentary has become dialogic rather than monologic; it is divided between two voices, each trying to impose its reading or gaze:

LAWYER: Certain commentators have pointed out that the Man came to the door of his own free will.
K.: And we're supposed to swallow all that? . . . What a miserable conclusion! It turns lying into a universal principle. (167)

K. and the lawyer confront each other before the image, before the screen or canvas, *vor der Leinwand*. As though they were engaging in a Japanese *benshi* competition. Or a battle, a fistfight like that between the grandfather and the owner of the Apollo, like two boxers in a ring put up between the spectators and the film:

And with the film running on top of them they fought on. . . . Grandfather and Herr Theilhaber were both red in the face. They panted for breath. They looked out into the Apollo; they looked at me. Then each tried to push the other off the stage. But the other fought back. Each *said with his eyes* [*sagte mit seinem Augen*; my emphasis]: He's gone mad, just look at him! Thank God, it was the matinée. There were only five people there. They were all watching the fight, not one of them was watching the film. (Hofmann, *Film Explainer*, 130)

When each punctuates (against) the punctuation of the other, when the film explainers go to war—a *war of points*—to impose their politics of the gaze, we no longer see anything. And yet this is what takes place in us, in the cinema that grandfather locates in our heads, in that schematizing imagination that forms our gaze.

Is the film explainer's lie, then, a universal principle, as K. says? He seems shocked, disgusted, by this. But in reality, he merely finds it reassuring, as do we with him. For as long as there are voices and explanations or counterexplanations, no matter how dishonest, the law of the image has yet to tighten its grip. It has yet to catch us in its grasp, this law that is neither true nor false, neither good nor dishonest [*ni bonne ni menteuse*], but gripping when it looks at us.

When its "points of gaze," as Lacan puts it, transfix us, nail us from the "side of things."[18]

13 / Punctuation and Politics, or The Dot above the i

What we must now consider is that punctuation, as phrasing, can be a force of resistance against the hold or mastery exercised by a power, for example, that of the image. And to approach the formidable political stakes in punctuation marks, I recall these lines from Leon Trotsky relating the events of autumn 1905 in Russia:

> The typesetters at Sytin's print-works in Moscow struck on September 19. They demanded a shorter working day and a higher piecework rate per 1,000 letters set, not excluding punctuation marks. This small event set off nothing more nor less than the all-Russian political strike—the strike which started over punctuation marks and ended by felling absolutism.[1]

What seems to astonish Trotsky is that there could be a consequential or cause-and-effect connection leading from punctuation marks to revolution. And we are certainly entitled to ask with him: How the devil does one go from a punctuation mark to politics? Is this not a perilous leap?

And yet Nietzsche did not hesitate to assert, in *The Case of Wagner*, that the emergence of the notion of phrasing participates in a movement in which "the power to decide falls into the hands of the masses."[2] For him, we recall, the proliferating development and expansion of punctuation even into the field of music clearly belongs to a general logic according to which the divisibility of the point, that is, its *overpunctuation*, threatens— or promises—to lead to a pulverulent dissemination. The "decline of the organizing power" that Nietzsche speaks of in his letter of 26 August 1888 to Carl Fuchs,[3] this luxuriance of the infinitesimal that sucks the life out of the whole, is what in fact leads, on the level of phrasing as much as on that of political power, to a becoming-sand, a becoming-granular and *puncti-form*. For this, as Nietzsche notes in a posthumous fragment from the spring of 1880, democracy and Christianity are primarily responsible:

> The more the feeling of unity with one's fellow man prevails, the more uniform they become, the stronger they will feel every difference to be immoral. Thus necessarily emerges the sand of humanity: all very similar, very small, very round. . . . Christianity and democracy have to this point led humanity the furthest on the path of this *metamorphosis into sand*.[4]

It is clear, then, if we follow Nietzsche, that the stakes of the point and punctuation are also those of sovereignty and sovereign decision.

• *On the one hand*, the point is the indivisible—atomic or atomystic— One that is the paradigm of the absolute monarch. Imagine the king par excellence: He is no doubt like that "creature droning on" that refers to itself as "it" (with no distinction between an I and a non-I), no doubt like the sovereign who governs the zero-dimensional country of the point in the Edwin Abbott's 1884 Victorian novel, written in the form of a geometrical satire and published under the title *Flatland*:

> That Point . . . is himself his own World, his own Universe; of any other than himself he can form no conception; . . . he has no cognizance even of the number Two; nor has he a thought of Plurality; for he is himself this One and All, being really Nothing.[5]

The absolute sovereign is thus the point.

Which is to say, nothing, in effect, since *Pointland*, the country of the point, is nothing but a "non-dimensional Gulf." Accordingly, sovereignty is that punctiformity that, as though in a vacuum, literally overpunctuates the highest instance or peak [*pointe*] of decision with a point or dot, as Hegel writes in his *Elements of the Philosophy of Right*:

> A frequent objection to monarchy is that it makes the affairs of the state subject to contingency—since the monarch may be ill-educated or unworthy of holding the highest office [*Spitze*, that is, the peak (*pointe*)]—and that it is absurd for such a situation to be regarded as rational. But this objection is based on the invalid assumption that the monarch's particular character is of vital importance. In a fully organized state, it is only a question of the highest instance [or peak (*pointe*): *Spitze* again] of formal decision, and all that is required in a monarch is someone to say "yes" and to dot the "i"; for the supreme

office [the head (*pointe*): *Spitze* once again] should be such that the particular character of its occupant is of no significance.[6]

At the head of the state, at the highest point of its verticality, erected in the image of the letter *i*, the sovereign monarch is the dot [*point*] added on, the dot that affirms, confirms, marks, and signs the punctiformity of the peak [*pointe*] as such, a bit like a Perekladin clinging to the peak of his upside down exclamation point.

• But *on the other hand*, if the monarch is thus an overpunctuation that has been added on, it is because its punctiformity is detachable or pros- thetic, as it were: It is already divided or divisible. Thus, from the start and structurally it loses its point, like a beheaded pyramid, that monument of monuments Tristram's father talks about in the speech he gives on the oc- casion of the death of one of his sons.

That is why the overpunctuating punctuation of the dot above the *i* is also precisely what deposes sovereignty by cutting it down, even decapi- tating it.[7]

This oscillation of punctuating force between sovereign decision and its blunting no doubt forms the center or matrix of the countless anec- dotes that fill the history of punctuation and the infinite metaphors to which its marks give rise. It's worth recalling a few.

We have heard the former President of the United States, George W. Bush, declare, with regard to the war in Iraq:

> When this chapter of history will be written . . . it's going to be a
> comma—the Iraqis voted, comma, and the United States of America
> understood that Iraq was a central front in the war on terror and
> helped this young democracy flourish.[8]

One could inscribe such a formulation in a veritable political history of the comma across the centuries, a history that remains to be written. I think in particular of what has been said about the calculated absence of a comma in a sentence that the English General Thomas Fairfax inserted at the bottom of the death warrant for King Charles I or of a similar anecdote passed along by Voltaire on the subject of the papacy's condemnation of the theologian Michel de Bay, the precursor of Jansenism.[9] Other punc- tuation marks, of course, should not be omitted, from the "final period" that Hiroshima was supposed to have been for World War II to Adorno's reflections on the quotation marks that in Marx already announce the totalitarian appropriation of his thinking.[10]

It will come as no surprise, then, that a project to reform punctuation should be a part of the political utopia of Charles Fourier, who in the postface to his *Nouveau monde industriel et sociétaire* wrote:

> In addition to the alphabet of letters, it would be necessary to cre-
> ate that of punctuation, which should contain the same number of
> marks; why the French have only seven punctuation marks, that
> is, , ; : . ! ?), is unknown. . . . I started a work on the gamut of punctu-
> ation; I had pushed it to 25 marks, supported with examples indicat-
> ing the foolishness and ambiguity of our current marks; I lost this
> work before it was completed and I have not started it again since. Let
> us observe, on this subject, that the first of our marks, the lowest one,
> called the *comma*, should be differentiated in at least four ways for its
> different meanings to be appreciated; the expression of its infinitely
> varying acceptations with a single mark is confusing: it is the height
> of disorder. It is the same with the other marks; they accumulate 3 or
> 4 meanings: civilized punctuation is a real chaos.[11]

More than a century later, Paul Valéry echoed this diagnosis in his *Cahiers* when in 1944 he noted that "our punctuation is vicious." Also contemplating a reform of punctuation marks along the lines of the musical model ("Why not marks like in music? . . . Marks for speed, for strong accenting—stops of differing lengths. Marks for 'vivace,' 'solemn,' staccato, playful . . ."), Valéry writes that "if we were truly 'revolutionaries' (like the Russians) we would dare to question the conventions of language."[12]

Punctuation, then, does not merely lend itself exemplarily to being interpreted in political terms but is also considered, over and over, to have political stakes by itself and as such.

Why?

In "Theory of Points," the sixth book of his *Logics of Worlds*, Alain Badiou maintains that a punctuating point relates above all to a theory of decision, for by a point, he writes, we must understand "what confronts the global situation with singular choices" that involve "the 'yes' and the 'no.'"[13] In short, for Badiou a point exists when "the totality of the world is at stake in a game of heads or tails" (400). And that is why he can assert that "Kierkegaard identifies existence with what we call a point," that is, "the test of a point" (427) that always makes a decision, since it is always a question, there, of "filtering the infinite through the Two" (437), of making the infinite pass through the alternative of an "either . . . or."

Badiou's "Theory of Points" is a war machine—most of his examples or applications are inscribed in reflections on war—directed against what he calls "democratic materialism" as the generator of "atonic worlds" (420), worlds that are not tense because they are without points, without the binary tests of decision. Worlds inhabited by "pointless" beings (443) of whom Bartleby, the character in the Melville story by the same name, seems to be the paradigm. Deconstructing the duality of a decisionism of binary choice, Bartleby "would prefer not to." He is, for Badiou— who dispenses with him, by the way, in three lines (400)—"betrayal" personified.

A stigmatology worthy of the name, one that listens attentively to all the phenomena of overpunctuation that I have raised to this point, must radically complicate such a "Theory of Points."[14] For every dual decision amounts to saying yes (or no) not only to one of the two branches of the alternative, but also *to the form of the alternative itself* (to the "either/ or," the "yes or no," as such), so that a doubling of the point itself, that is, a doubling of punctiformity as the supposed instance of the Two, takes place in that decision.

Put differently, where Badiou sees one point, there are (at least) two. Where for him it is a question of saying yes or no (this is essentially his definition of the point), stigmatology, instead, will auscultate the construction of this point, hearing in it the punctuation that is doubled by a yes (or no) that will also and at the same time have said yes (or no) *to the form of the yes-or-no*. In short, what Badiou's "Theory of Points" does not theorize is punctuation as being *always already* an overpunctuation.

14 / Final Survey

Walter Benjamin knew better than anyone how to seize upon the auscultatory, that is, the dotting and overpunctuating, dimension of every *rereading*. In a fragment titled "Lesen" ("Reading"), he writes (and I translate these admirable lines as closely as I can):

> There are people—and among them some possess an entire library—
> who never really approach a book [*niemals recht an ein Buch her-
> ankommen*], for they never read anything a second time [*weil sie
> nichts zum zweiten Mal lesen*]. And yet it is only then that, as though
> sounding a wall by knocking [*wie klopfend ein Gemäuer absucht*], one
> in spots comes upon a hollow echo [*einen hohlen Widerhall*] . . . and
> finds treasures that the previous reader—the one we were—buried
> there.[1]

Yes, to sound or survey. For it is *your* turn to play now, you who have
just read the long, sinuous phrase formed by the chapters through which
you are at this very moment arriving here, at this almost terminal point •
where it is *your* turn to take stock [*faire le point*], to punctuate and evaluate, to auscultate and estimate what has come before, point by point.

This is why this somewhat mad (but banal at that same time—it is what
almost all writing does or believes it must do at the moment of concluding) thought comes to me. It is why this no doubt impossible or somewhat perverse idea springs to my mind. I could, I tell myself, accompany
you in a recapitulation that, like an accountant's checklist already used by
Egyptian scribes a few millennia ago, would try to review everything we
have gone through, you and I. I could escort you and even—the height

of the perversion or pulsion of mastery—delineate your inventory in advance, mark out your checklist by providing blanks, empty spaces, Tristramesque holes in the text that,

far from simply being there for the reader to draw a portrait in as he or she pleases or to fill with all the curses and punctuating exclamations he or she wants, would be so many textual hollows, so many cavities that I would reserve in the preformed form we know them by today, that of a simple alternative:

Yes ❏ or No ❏,

whose implicit injunction would be: Check off your preference; fill the square you choose; in short, conform to a "heads or tails" that, not without recalling a certain "Theory of Points," constantly extends its hold throughout the generalized practice of surveys.

Thus, you could mark your points of agreement or disagreement—and (why not), if you want to say neither yes nor no, your indifference:

Must punctuation be reformed, as Fourier and Valéry wished?
Yes ❏ No ❏ (no opinion ❏).

 You could mark your preferences, say what you wish or not, what you like or don't like, as we now tend to do all the time and for everything, for example on Facebook.[2] You could count the points, **rubric** or <u>underline</u> as you please, add all the distinctions ● ˙ that might occur to you as well, by initialing them—why not—(like a Symmachus). In short, you could take your turn at *overpunctuating*, engaging in the most recent technical applications and variations of what Heidegger called "thinking in values" [*das Denken in Werten*], which has been generalized to the point that our existence, each instant of our experience, tends to become a permanent survey, a constant evaluation that for this very reason also and always more and more sinks into equivalence or indifference.

According to the logic to which Nietzsche was the first to give the so simple and yet so difficult name of nihilism, according to this logic that Heidegger analyzed and formalized in all of its monotonous and infinite power, to think in values is in fact to punctuate:

Once valuative thought [*der Wertgedanke*] has come on the scene, it must also be admitted that values "are" only where there is calculation [*wo gerechnet wird*]. . . . To speak about "values in themselves" is either thoughtlessness or counterfeiting [*entweder eine Gedankenlosigkeit oder eine Falschmünzerei*], or both. "Value," according to its essence, is "viewpoint" [*"Wert" ist seinem Wesen nach "Gesichtspunkt"*]. There are viewpoints only for a seeing that points [*für ein Sehen, das punktiert*] and calculates by means of "points" [*nach "Punkten" rechnen muß*].[3]

This is what Carl Schmitt repeats in his own way by speaking of the "punctualism of the thinking in values" (*Punktualismus des Wertdenkens*), asserting that "the philosophy of values is a philosophy of the point" (*die Wert-Philosophie ist eine Punkt-Philosophie*).[4]

So, what do you think? Verify, count, check off, as the administrative scribes did in ancient Egypt, and see if you agree on all points. Or would you perhaps say that it depends, that we have to see, depending on the points of view, that we can always discuss, phrase, interpret, explain—in short, *evaluate*?

Yet this is anything but a simple matter of opinion. Or rather, and more precisely, opinion itself is not a matter of opinion, far from it: It is a construction that is a matter of a technology of pointing and punctuation. Measuring and shaping opinion are in fact inscribed in a (Nietzschean) history of the punctuating thinking of values, the same thinking that has also produced the philosophical deployment of auscultation, of visible or invisible quotation marks, as well as of phrasing—*Phrasierung*, that "ugly term," as Nietzsche put it, hearing in it the heralding of the overthrow of sovereign values, and even the becoming-sand of Christian-Democratic humanity.

Opinion polls like the ones we are familiar with today of course saw the light of day more than a half-century after *The Case of Wagner* and in a very different context, the United States of the mid-'30s. But what spreads with them is precisely calculability and thus the general convertibility of values and evaluations, in a trajectory that is everywhere heralded in Nietzsche's work.

Without getting into the factual details of the invention of surveys, one can say that the book published by George Gallup and Saul Forbes Rae in 1940, *The Pulse of Democracy*,[5] testifies to what is at stake in configuring public opinion into a statistically measurable phenomenon (which it had never been to that point), that is, transforming it into a series of punctuated points of view that, as Heidegger would say, will henceforth be *calculable in terms of points*. It is indeed a question for Gallup of arriving at "a more reliable measure of the pulse of democracy" (14), of better auscultating it or, if you prefer, of feeling its *punctum saliens* with greater precision.

> The kind of public opinion implied in the democratic ideal is tangible and dynamic. It springs from many sources deep in the day-to-day experience of individuals who constitute the political public. . . . It believes in the value of every individual's contribution to political life. Public opinion, in this sense, is the pulse of democracy. (8)

The opinion whose pulse is being measured thus is constantly gaining or losing points. The opinion that is supposed to be the result of countless springs flowing from the everyday, that in its perpetual oscillations is supposed to represent the values added on, the cumulative points of view of all the singular or punctiform individuals that form it, is at all times punctuated or measured on a scale.[6] In the background of the birth of the modern poll is what one can call, adopting Carl Schmitt's term, a *punctualism*.

But for Gallup, the punctuating evaluation in which pollsters engage should also, ideally, be *constant*, that is, similar to a sort of incessant oversight or surveillance:

> Elections can never be the sole channel for the expression of public opinion, although they remain, at particular times, probably the best single measure of public opinion obtainable. But there is still a need, even in the best of representative systems, for keeping the legislator *in constant touch* with public opinion. (*Pulse of Democracy*, 21, emphasis added)

Public opinion should thus be subjected to a hypervigilant monitoring of its pulse, for it is a question not only of making heard thus "the voices of the people," but also and perhaps most of all of ensuring that these voices *hear themselves*: "For public opinion can be a satisfactory guide only if we can hear it and, what is equally important, if it can hear itself" (14).

The poll, as the continuous statement of the minute pulsating variations of the body of supposedly common values, tends to become the micropercussion of an infinitesimal auscultation. In the extreme attention it gives to the slightest jump in the democratic *punctum saliens*, it is like the musical punctuation Nietzsche distrusted so. It *overphrases* the sociopolitical text. It produces its infinite phraseological fragmentation, which for Gallup as for certain of his predecessors would nevertheless herald a new and "more efficient" phase of democracy: its perpetual showing of itself.[7]

Here more than ever, in what one might again describe with Nietzsche as the luxuriance of small things being enlivened, punctuating hyperarticulation becomes an overpunctuation in which tallying punctuates itself. In fact, as Gallup notes, not without a certain bafflement:

> We are now witnessing a paradoxical but unavoidable phenomenon —the polls of public opinion are themselves becoming an issue of public opinion. . . . During the short space of four years [*The Pulse of Democracy* appeared in 1940; the first polls date from the end of 1935], a considerable body of criticism has been directed at this effort to take the pulse of democracy. (213)

These lines open the third part of *The Pulse of Democracy*, titled "Evaluations." In which what is evaluated in being overpunctuated is thus punctuating evaluation itself.

Opinion and poll, in the sense in which we are here listening to them as symptoms, are not at all a strictly sociological matter. Or better: If it is a question of sociology, it is in the sense in which, for Gabriel Tarde, there was a "universal sociological point of view" according to which "every thing is a society" and "every phenomenon is a social fact."[8] As for overpunctuation—and here we are, back to it *in fine*—it is far, very far, from being a specifically typographical or syntactic question: Overpunctuation in fact falls under a *general* stigmatology.

To overpunctuate [*surponctuer*]: This word, this verb, has indeed constantly stuck its nose out in the preceding pages. Since it insists on resurfacing, we must no doubt grant it the place, the importance, of a major motif in the stigmatology I have tried to sketch out. And what we should thus ask ourselves as we conclude is quite simply this: What, in this recurring term, does the prefix *over* [sur] mean?

There are several possible answers.

❏ *Over* [*sur*] is first of all the aftereffect of a retrospective punctuation (a retrauditive one, we could also say, with the beautiful verb we come upon in Heidegger's *The Principle of Reason*, *zurückhören*, in mind), a punctuation whose movement is none other than the retroaction Lacan speaks of in translating Freudian *Nachträglichkeit*, that is, that of the needle of a mattress maker who stitches backwards.[9] ❏ *Over* then designates the hyperbole of a hyperpunctuation that, by dint of detailed articula-tion, atomizes, pulverizes, and granularizes phrases and forms, moving toward what Nietzsche named a "metamorphosis into sand" in the nihil-ist desert.

❑ *To overpunctuate* is to re-mark, to mark with a supplemental mark: It is to underline or highlight the existing punctuation, for example, by signing it (as Asterius did after punctuating his copy of Virgil). ❑ But *to overpunctuate* thus, to add signs over and above, in excess, is also to mask the punctuation mark by making it opaque with the remark that is superimposed on it: The admonisher and the film explainer (❦ Caution! They can always be internalized ☞ in the image or the imagination) do nothing else when they point to themselves in showing their showing (*das Aufzeigen des Zeigens*, Hegel would say).

Is punctuating therefore overpunctuating?
Yes ❑ No ❑ (No opinion ❑)

❑ *Over* names the leaping movement that causes a jump in level, that causes the movement from the level of the narrative [*récit*] to that of the recitative, from the story to the way this story is recounted. When Hegel speaks of the point that has its actuality in time rather than space, when he mentions points of life (*Lebenspunkte*) that emerge in the sea or the thousand eyes that one sees appear on the surface of a painting, these points, as well as so many others, are not only mentioned or described; they do not merely represent a key moment, a remarkable passage in the narrative of the dialectic of nature or art; they are also, in addition, punc-tuating points that mark the transition toward a new chapter, toward a new section or rubric, in short, toward a new period or limb in the specu-lative phrase of thinking. ❑ But *over* is also and perhaps above all the leap or bounce of pulsation, elasticity: It is the discontraction of the systole supervening upon the diastole and vice versa; it is, as Hegel says, freedom at once *in* and *from* matter—where the possibility of phrasing, vocalizing, begins then. ❑ And this is why *over* also indicates, of course, the gap that makes stigmatology possible as the discourse *on* [*sur*] punctuation marks as such.

But to be sure, ❑ *over*, finally, is the oscillation, the vibration, between all the preceding meanings of the prefix *over*, between all the points, all the entries or boxes in the list that you have just gone over again.

Check one of those boxes ✗, select this one or that ✓, you'll see that right away another will probably turn up [*se pointe*] •

Notes

1 / Stigmatology

I had the good fortune to consult a draft translation of this chapter by Will Bishop in preparing my own translation. It has benefited immeasurably from Bishop's work, which I acknowledge here gratefully.—JP.

1. "The ring becomes an allegory of whatever you do in life," declares Scorsese in an interview in 1991 ("What the Streets Mean," *Martin Scorsese: Interviews*, ed. Peter Brunette [Jackson: University Press of Mississippi, 1999], 167), before suggesting that "people just living daily life" are, so to speak, structurally "in the ring."

2. See Thiery Groensteen, *Système de la bande dessinée* (Paris: Presses universitaires de France, 1999): "It is . . . first of all in the interstitial blank (called, depending on the author, 'intericonic space,' 'interboxes,' 'inter-images'—or even 'gouttière,' a transposition of the English *gutter*)—that the reader recognizes the virtue of separation." A few lines earlier, the author introduced this comparison, which would be worth analyzing closely: "In this regard, the vignette frame plays a role analogous to that of punctuation marks in language (including the elementary mark that is the blank separating two words), these marks that cut up, within a *continuum*, the pertinent unities" (54). See also Claude-Françoise Brunon, "L'Entr'Images," *Europe* 720 (April 1989), which was devoted to *La Bande déssinée*.

3. Thanks to Laura Odello for opening my eyes to this instantaneous irruption of Tyler, which is repeated several times in the first part of the film. During an interview with Gavin Smith ("Inside Out," *Film Comment* 35, no. 5 [1999], 58–66), David Fincher explains that there are "five or six shots" in which Tyler appears "in one frame."

4. For example, there is the *sacred stigmatology*, that is, the punctuation of the Hebrew text of the Bible, to which the Scottish Reverend Thomas Boston devoted a treatise (*Tractatus stigmologicus hebraeo-biblicus* [Amsterdam, 1738]) and which he mentions several times in his memoirs (*Memoirs of the Life, Time, and Writings, of The Reverend and Learned Thomas Boston* [Edinburgh: Printed by A. Murray and J. Cochran, for W. Anderson, 1776], 313 and 37 of the Appendix). More recently, the

theologian and medievalist Martin Hubert has compiled a collection of texts on punctuation, from Aristotle to the twelfth century, titled *Corpus stigmatologicum* (in the *Archivum latinitatis Medii Aevi*, 37, 1970).

5. The—no doubt apocryphal—anecdote about Victor Hugo is cited just about everywhere in popularizing books on the art of punctuation, such as the best seller by Lynne Truss, *Eats, Shoots and Leaves: The Zero Tolerance Approach to Punctuation* (New York: Gotham Books, 2004), 136. In her recent *Esthétique de la ponctuation* (Paris: Gallimard, 2012), Isabelle Serça analyzes the punctuation of the page or work in Proust (147–51). She also considers (138–39) certain paradoxical arrangements—what she calls an "oxymoronic punctuation"—like this closing parenthesis in *La Route des Flandres* that Claude Simon precedes with a colon that in a sense traverses it: ". . . and sitting down completely, inhaling an endless puff of smoke until he felt it reaching all the way to the bottom of his lungs, exhaling it as slowly as possible, saying:) 'So he was here, on that road.'" Claude Simon, *The Flanders Road*, trans. Richard Howard (London: Calder, 1985), 164. On Cummings's punctuation, see the fine book by Isabelle Alfandary, *E. E. Cummings ou la minuscule lyrique* (Paris: Belin, 2002). Jacques Demarcq ("Ce jeune point d'interrogation," in the issue of *Traverses* on *Génie de la ponctuation* [43]; Paris: Centre Pompidou, 110) suggests that we name the proliferation of exclamation points and other signs, even into the interior of the lexeme, "overpunctuation": This is the case—to pick one example among others—in the Cummings poem titled "(fea," where the word *softer* is written *so / ! f ! / te / / r?*, as though abysses were opening in it as we spell it out, reading it slowly (E. E. Cummings, *Complete Poems, 1904–1962*, ed. George J. Firmage [New York: Liveright, 1973], 653).

6. Walter Murch, *In the Blink of an Eye: A Perspective on Film Editing* (Los Angeles: Silman-James Press, 1995), 62–63. In her memoirs, the British writer Hannah More recalls a conversation with Capability Brown: "He compared his art to literary composition. Now *there*, said he, pointing his finger, I make a comma and *there*, pointing to another spot where a more decided turn is proper, I make a colon" (*Memoirs of the Life and Correspondence of Mrs. Hannah More* [New York: Harper and Brothers, 1837], 2:155). Thanks to Eduardo Cadava for pointing this passage out to me.

7. One would need to read in detail everything Adorno says in his magnificent little text titled "Punctuation Marks" (in *Notes to Literature*, vol. 1, trans. Shierry Weber Nicholsen [New York: Columbia University Press, 1991], 91). The Danish comedian Victor Borge (1909–2000), who emigrated to the United States to flee Nazism, was especially famous for his show on "phonetic punctuation," in which he pretended to read aloud, giving each punctuation mark an onomatopoeia that was somewhat . . . invasive. As for Gad Elmaleh, he asks, in one of the most hilarious scenes in *Papa est en haut* (2008): "If we spoke in life like we speak in text messages, how would we make *smileys*?" These *smileys*—or emoticons, as they are also called—are beginning to appear in literature (see in particular Lauren Myracle's young adult novel *ttyl* [for "talk to you later"], published by Amulent Books in 2004 and composed entirely of text messages), and even in essays (see Jennifer DeVere Brody, *Punctuation: Art, Politics, and Play* [Durham, N.C.: Duke University Press, 2008], 134 ff.).

8. Anton Chekhov, "The Exclamation Mark (A Christmas Story)," in *The Exclamation Mark*, trans. Rosamund Bartlett (London: Hesperus, 2008), 4. [Hereafter cited parenthetically. The translation is sometimes very slightly modified.—Trans.] The images that follow are taken from the beautiful adaptation of the story in a comic strip by

Olga Ryahovskaya. I would like to thank her for allowing me to reproduce them (her work can be consulted at oly-rrr.deviantart.com/).

9. On some of Lacan's works, to which I will return at length, Samuel Weber notes: "At the heart of the subject is a certain punctuation" (*Return to Freud: Jacques Lacan's Dislocation of Psychoanalysis* [Cambridge: Cambridge University Press, 1991], 97).

2 / From the *Rubrica* to the *Smiley*: A Portable History

1. Edgar Allan Poe, "The Gold-Bug," in *The House of Usher and Other Writings: Poems, Tales, Essays, and Reviews*, ed. David Galloway (London: Penguin Classics, 2003), 261.

2. Honoré de Balzac, *Colonel Chabert*, trans. Carol Cosman (Toronto: Penguin, 1997), 2.

3. Jean Winand, "La Ponctuation avant la ponctuation: L'Organisation du message écrit dans l'Egypte pharaonique," in *À qui appartient la ponctuation?*, ed. Jean-Marc Defays, Laurence Rosier, and Françoise Tilkin (Paris: Duculot, 1998): "According to the tradition, the habit of punctuating a text goes back to Aristophanes of Byzantium or to his disciple Dionysius Thrax. In fact, it is likely that these scholars did not invent punctuation, but that they systematized and refined a technique that was still embryonic. . . . It is difficult to assert with certainty that the Alexandrians picked up punctuation from the Egyptians, but it is very probable, if only because of the permanent contacts between the Greeks in Egypt and the Egyptians" (175).

4. Winand also mentions "the discovery made in Amarna of Babylonian mythological texts punctuated by Egyptian scribes": "Again points are written in red ink on tablets. Here is a remarkable fact: the tablets were composed in Babylonia and not in Egypt. The punctuation was therefore done *later* [my emphasis and rubricking again], in Egypt, and in the same way as on papyrus, in red ink, while Acadian writing is done by pressing upon a tablet of fresh clay. The points are written above the line, as in the Egyptian practice. The points in these tablets isolate very small units: the verb, a preposition followed by its object, the verb preceded by negation, etc. General consensus is that this is a scholarly use intended to make it easier to learn to read Acadian, the diplomatic language of the time. It will be noted that this practice dates from the eighteenth dynasty, that is, that it is contemporary with the extension of the use of punctuation in Egyptian texts properly speaking" (174).

5. "The point perhaps finds its origin in a kind of pointing used in the accounts and records of El-Lahun, a group of archival documents dating to the twelfth dynasty. If this hypothesis proves correct, the point . . . was invented in administrative circles" (173–74). Winand adds in a note that, on certain documents, "the point seems to be intended to maintain the justification of the column when there is nothing to be noted there." The practice of the *rubrica* also seems to issue from techniques of calculation: "Historically, the rubric seems to be an administrative invention that served to highlight dates and totals in accounting. Thus, in numerous literary manuscripts one finds the numbers, dates, even references of an accounting character (such as the word . . . *total*) regularly rubricked, probably out of habit. The oldest rubricked literary manuscripts date to the Middle Empire, but the use of the two-color process is older. It is used in administrative texts from the fourth . . . and fifth dynasties on. . . . Moreover, the use of red ink in a still older era is suggested by the existence of scribes' palettes dating to the first dynasty that already contained two cavities, one for black ink, the

other for red, or by certain representations in the Ancient Empire showing the scribe with two brushes. The use of red ink was only introduced into literary texts later" (168).

6. This *scriptio* or *scriptura continua* seems to have been the consequence of the introduction of vowels into the alphabet. See Paul Saenger, *Space between Words: The Origins of Silent Reading* (Stanford, Calif.: Stanford University Press, 1997): "Before the introduction of vowels to the Phoenician alphabet, all the ancient languages of the Mediterranean world . . . were written with word separation by either space, points, or both in conjunction. After the introduction of vowels, word separation was no longer necessary to eliminate an unacceptable level of ambiguity. . . . The adoption of vowels and of *scriptura continua* went hand in hand. The ancient writings of Mesopotamia, Phoenicia, and Israel did not employ vowels, so separation between words was retained. . . . While the very earliest Greek inscriptions were written with separation by interpuncts, points placed at midlevel between words, Greece soon thereafter became the first ancient civilization to employ *scriptura continua*. The Romans, who borrowed their letter forms and vowels from the Greeks, maintained the earlier Mediterranean tradition of separating words by points far longer than the Greeks, but they, too, after a scantily documented period of six centuries, discarded word separation as superfluous and substituted *scriptura continua* for interpunct-separated script" (9–10). As Saenger recalls, *scriptura continua* was long considered "a retrograde development in human history" (10), a regression in the ease of reading; he emphasizes, however, that "the Roman Empire, which for a time enjoyed the widespread use of interpunct-separated Latin script with vowels, chose to discard that form of writing for *scriptura continua*" (10). I thank Helen Tartar for having pointed out Paul Saenger's beautiful work.

7. Malcolm Parkes, *Pause and Effect: An Introduction to the History of Punctuation in the West* (Berkeley: University of California Press, 1993), 14.

8. Theodor Adorno, "Punctuation Marks," in *Notes to Literature*, vol. 1, trans. Shierry Weber Nicholsen (New York: Columbia University Press, 1991), 91.

9. Jean-Léonor Le Gallois de Grimarest, *Traité du récitatif, dans la lecture, dans l'action publique, dans la déclamation, et dans le chant: Avec un traité des accens, de la quantité, & de la ponctuation* (Paris: Jaques le Fevre and Pierre Ribou, 1707), 47–48.

10. Throughout this passage, both "mark" and "dot" translate the French "point," which can also be rendered as "period."—Trans.

11. Jean-Jacques Rousseau, *Essay on the Origin of Languages and Writings Related to Music*, vol. 7 of *The Collected Writings of Rousseau*, trans. and ed. John T. Scott (Hanover, N.H.: University Press of New England, 1998), 300.

12. Well before the introduction of the *smiley* into email messages in 1982, the satirist Ambrose Bierce, author of a *Devil's Dictionary*, proposed, in 1887, what he called the "snigger point," that is, a parenthesis simply turned horizontal to represent a laughing mouth (see Jonathon Keats, *Virtual Words: Language on the Edge of Science and Technology* [Oxford: Oxford University Press, 2011], 125). Bazin's "intonation marks" are reproduced in Nina Catach, *La Ponctuation* (Paris: Presses universitaires de France, 1994), 10. On Alcanter de Brahm's irony mark, see Pierre Schoentjes, "Ponctuer l'ironie," in *À qui appartient la ponctuation?* ed. Jean-Marc Defays, Laurence Rosier, and Françoise Tilkin (Paris: Duculot, 1998), 310. After having mentioned the "vocative mark," Rousseau also seems to dream of a punctuation capable of marking irony: "Why, for example, do we not have a vocative mark? The question mark we do have was much less necessary, for one sees by construction alone whether or not a question is being asked, at least in our language. *Are you coming* and *you are coming* are not the

same thing. But how does one distinguish in writing a man who is being mentioned from one being addressed? Here is a real equivocation, which the vocative point would have removed. The same equivocation occurs in irony, when accent does not make it felt" (300).

3 / The Point of (No) Monument, or Tristram's Cut

1. Laurence Sterne, *The Life and Opinions of Tristram Shandy, Gentleman*, ed. Ian Campbell Ross (Oxford: Oxford University Press, 1982), 423.

2. Which would therefore have to be called, as Louis Marin suggested, "autobio-thanatographic." See *La Voix excommuniée: Essais de mémoire* (Paris: Galilée, 1981), especially 37: "autobiothanatography, in which the subject appropriates itself and identifies with itself from the point of an unspeakable double limit, its birth and death, of two statements, 'I was born' and 'I died.'" Two statements that for Marin form a "double impossible cogito" (38). I must also refer here to Philippe Lacoue-Labarthe's beautiful pages in "Echo of the Subject" [in *Typography: Mimesis, Philosophy, Politics*, ed. Christopher Fynsk, trans. Barbara Harlow (Stanford, Calif.: Stanford University Press, 1998), 179 passim] on autobiography as allothanatography or heterothanatography.

3. "What I have called the 'button tie' [*point de capiton*]," Lacan wrote, is that "by which the signifier stops the otherwise indefinite sliding of signification" (Jacques Lacan, "Subversion of the Subject and the Dialectic of Desire in the Freudian Unconscious," in *Écrits: The First Complete Edition in English*, trans. Bruce Fink (New York: W. W. Norton, 2005), 681). I will return later to the metaphor of buttoning that regulates this concept and that Lacan borrows from upholstery. On punctuation in *Tristram Shandy*, see Roger B. Moss, "Sterne's Punctuation," *Eighteenth-Century Studies* 15, no. 2 (1981–82): 179–200. [Translations of Lacan typically render *point de capiton* as either *quilting point* or *button tie*, both entirely correct. Throughout this translation, the two will be combined in order to maintain the emphasis on the punctuating *point*, which is also suggested in the figure of the button. The phrase *button point* also has the advantage of capturing the play on buttoning and unbuttoning.—Trans.]

4. There is in fact, in the so-called Geneva manuscript of the *Confessions*, a short page preceding the text's well-known *incipit* ("I have resolved on an enterprise which has no precedent . . ."). It is a sort of foreword—a "before-the-first word," Jacques Derrida wrote, commenting on its singular call ("Typewriter Ribbon: Without Ink (2)," in *Without Alibi*, ed. and trans. Peggy Kamuf (Stanford, Calif.: Stanford University Press, 2002), 142–43. There Rousseau declares: "This is the only portrait of a man drawn precisely from nature and in all its truth, that exists and that will probably ever exist. Whoever you are whom my destiny or my confidence has made the arbiter of the fate of this *cahier*, I beseech you by my misfortunes, by your entrails and in the name of the whole human race not to annihilate a unique and useful work, which can serve as the first piece of comparison for the study of man, a study that is certainly yet to be begun, and not to remove from the honor of my memory the only certain document [*monument*] of my character that has not been disfigured by my enemies." In Jean-Jacques Rousseau, *The Confessions*, trans. J. M. Cohen (New York: Penguin Books, 1953), 17. [Peggy Kamuf notes, "This paragraph from the Geneva Manuscript is omitted in Cohen's translation of *Confessions*." She translates it from Rousseau, *Oeuvres complètes*, vol. 1, ed. Bernard Gagnebin et al. (Paris: Gallimard, 1959), 3.—Trans.]

5. The answer to the question Tristram, in chapter 2, poses to the captain of the boat that takes him from Dover to Calais ("Pray Captain, quoth I, as I was going down into the cabin, is a man never overtaken by *Death* in this passage?" [386]) no doubt resides in the brief considerations in chapter 4 on writing and horse racing, when Tristram mentions "all who have *wrote and gallop'd*—or who have *gallop'd and wrote*, which is a different way still; or who for more expedition than the rest, have *wrote-galloping* which is the way I do at present" (387–88). In fact, it is only toward the end of the fifth volume (chapter 42), after so many pages of writing at a gallop, that Tristram can say (provisionally, of course), "I had left Death, the lord knows——and He only—how far behind me——" (428).

6. I borrow this word from Jacques Derrida in *Spurs: Nietzsche's Styles/Éperons: Les Styles de Nietzsche*, trans. Barbara Harlow (Chicago: University of Chicago Press, 1979): "Perhaps at this point one ought to interrogate—and unbutton . . ." (59, translation modified—Trans.). Let us recall also, as do Philippe Lacoue-Labarthe and Jean-Luc Nancy in *The Title of the Letter: A Reading of Lacan*, trans. François Raffoul and David Pettigrew (Albany: State University of New York Press, 1992), that "the anchoring point [*point de capiton*] is presented by Lacan as *mythical*: there is no signification which is not always already sliding outside of its alleged proper meaning" (54–55). Nancy and Lacoue-Labarthe cite Lacan himself, in book 5 of the *Seminar* (*Les Formations de l'inconscient; Formations of the Unconscious* [1958–59] [Paris: Seuil, 1998]): "The pinning of which I speak, the quilting point, is only a matter of myth, for no one has ever been able to pin a signification to a signifier. On the other hand, what one can do is pin a signifier to a signifier" (196).

4 / (Un)Pointings

The title of this chapter, "Épointages," invokes at once bringing something to a point, making it pointed, and removing that point, making blunt, as the author points out in the final note to the chapter. It might also be rendered by the two senses of the English *to top*.—Trans.

1. On the translation of Lacan's *point de capiton* as "button point," see note 3 in chapter 3.—Trans.

2. "Point" here translates the French *point*, which could also be rendered as "dot" or "period."—Trans.

3. It must be noted that this paragraph is introduced by considerations of the attachment or connection ("*ligament*") formed in the looks exchanged between Tristram's uncle (Toby), Lieutenant Le Fever, and his son: "——and that *ligament*, fine as it was,—was never broken.——" (343).

4. Tristram insists on the apparent arbitrariness of chaptering: "Is it not a shame to make two chapters of what passed in going down one pair of stairs? For we are got no farther yet than to the first landing, and there are fifteen more steps down to the bottom; and for aught I know, as my father and my uncle *Toby* are in a talking humour, there may be as many chapters as steps;—let that be as it will, Sir, I can no more help it drop the curtain, *Shandy*—I drop it——Strike a line here across the paper, *Tristram*— I strike it—and hey for a new chapter!" (225). And the twenty-fourth chapter of the fourth volume is missing: "—No doubt, Sir—there is a whole chapter wanting here— and a chasm of ten pages [in fact, in the English edition, there is a jump from page 240 to page 251] made in the book by it—but the book-binder is neither a fool, or a knave,

or a puppy—nor is the book a jot more imperfect, (at least upon that score)—but, on the contrary, the book is more perfect and complete by wanting the chapter, than having it. . . . I question first by the bye, whether the same experiment might not be made as successfully upon sundry other chapters——but there is no end, an' please your reverences, in trying experiments upon chapters—we have had enough of it—So there's an end of that matter" (251).

5. See the famous passage from the twenty-second chapter of volume 1: "My work is digressive, and it is progressive too,—and at the same time.

"This, Sir, is a very different story from that of the earth's moving round her axis, in her diurnal rotation, with her progress in her elliptick orbit which brings about the year, and constitutes that variety and vicissitude of seasons we enjoy;—though I own it suggested the thought,—as I believe the greatest of our boasted improvements and discoveries have come from some such trifling hints.

"Digressions, incontestably, are the sunshine; ——they are the life, the soul of reading;---take them out of this book for instance,--you might as we take the book along with them;—one cold eternal winter would reign in every page of it" (58).

6. It is a matter here of imagining the object of uncle Toby's love and "concupiscence," that is, the widow Wadman: "To conceive this right,—call for pen and ink— here's paper ready to your hand.——Sit down, Sir, paint her to your own mind——as like your mistress as you can——as unlike your wife as your conscience will let you—'tis all one to me——please but your own fancy in it" (376). And then after the blank page: "Thrice happy book! thou wilt have one page, at least, within thy covers, which MALICE will not blacken, and which IGNORANCE cannot misrepresent" (378). Later, in the ninth volume, as uncle Toby, accompanied by his faithful corporal Trim, enters Mrs. Wadman's house for the first time, we find two chapters (the eighteenth and nineteenth) reduced to a blank page, followed by a twentieth chapter that begins more or less thus: "——* * * * * . . ." (514). A way of translating the visitors' surprise, wonder?

7. As Roger B. Moss writes in his remarkable article, "The page is filled up rather than emptied, drowned by noise rather than left silent." Roger B. Moss, "Sterne's Punctuation," *Eighteenth-Century Studies* 15, no. 2 (1981–82): 191.

8. [The French translation the author cites has, in the place of the singular in Sterne, "les plus orgueilleuses pyramides," "the proudest pyramid*s*."—Trans.] This is analogous to what Lacan would say of the phallus, "the signifier of signifiers" (Jacques Lacan, "The Direction of the Treatment and the Principles of Its Power," in *Écrits: The First Complete Edition in English*, trans. Bruce Fink [New York: W. W. Norton, 2005], 526): "The signifier that is destined to designate meaning effects as a whole, insofar as the signifier conditions them by its presence as signifier" (Jacques Lacan, "The Signification of the Phallus," in *Écrits: The First Complete Edition in English*, trans. Bruce Fink [New York: W. W. Norton, 2005], 579); "the privileged signifier of this mark in which the role [*part*] of Logos is wedded to the advent of desire" (58).

9. The word *point* has a history similar to that of the word *pas*, as Auguste Scheler's *Dictionnaire d'étymologie française* (Paris: Firmin Didot, 1862) explains: "(1) PAS, movement of the legs, L[atin] *passus*. Expressing a small parcel of land, this word has served, like *goutte, point, mie* [in the sense of *miette*] to reinforce negation; 'je ne vois pas' is the lit[eral] equivalent of 'non video passum.' The Belgian linguist Marc Wilmet, in his *Grammaire critique du français* (Paris: Duculot, 2003), summarizes what linguists call the grammaticalization (or grammaticization) of the adverbs *pas*,

point, etc., that is, their transformation from the purely lexical words they were (nouns, substantives) into purely functional words expressing a merely grammatical relation (negation): "Evolution [. . .] will (1) dematerialize them, making them compatible with all verbs (e.g., *ne marcher mie*: not to walk; *ne boire point*: not to drink); (2) reduce them in number so that there remains today only *pas*, the already affected (or provincial) *point*, and a few preserved phrases: *ne souffler/piper mot* (not to breathe a word), *ne voir goutte* (not to see a thing)." The process that leads to the two values of *point*, in French, can therefore be described, according to linguists, as implying a *desemanticization* (abstraction of meaning) and an *extension* (use in new contexts).

10. "Épointer," as Charles Mauron puts it beautifully in his translation, rendering Yorick's word when he speaks of cutting—castrating—the pipes ("cut off spouts" [305]). *Épointer*, moreover, is a remarkable verb that has two exactly opposed uses, corresponding to two distinct entries in the *Littré*: (1) "to break the point, to blunt"; (2) "to make pointed, to sharpen."

5 / P.S.: On Restitching (Lacan vs. Derrida)

1. See Jacques Derrida, "Le Facteur de la Vérité," in *The Post Card: From Socrates to Freud and Beyond*, trans. Alan Bass (Chicago: University of Chicago Press, 1987).

2. Jacques Lacan, "The Function and Field of Speech and Language in Psychoanalysis," in *Écrits: The First Complete Edition in English*, trans. Bruce Fink (New York: Norton, 2006), 209. [Translations are sometimes very lightly modified.—Trans.]

3. Jacques Lacan, "The Subversion of the Subject and the Dialectic of Desire in the Freudian Unconscious," in *Écrits*. See also *Seminar III: The Psychoses*, trans. Russell Grigg, ed. Jacques-Alain Miller (New York: Norton, 1993): "It does have to be completed for one to know what is going on. The sentence only exists as completed and its sense comes to it retroactively" (262–63). [Translations are sometimes lightly modified.—Trans.]

4. Jean-Luc Nancy and Philippe Lacoue-Labarthe thus speak of "the *punctuation* of the subject" (*The Title of the Letter: A Reading of Lacan*, trans. François Raffoul and David Pettigrew [Albany: State University of New York Press, 1992], 70), which we should understand according to the double value, objective and subjective, of the genitive. Lacan himself, in the seminar we have already cited (*Psychoses*), notes that "the schema of the quilting point is essential in human experience" (268) before contemplating "managing to determine the minimum number of points of insertion between the signifier and signified necessary for a human being to be called normal, and which, when they are not established, or when they give way, make a psychosis" (268–69).

5. Aristotle, *Metaphysics*, in *The Complete Works of Aristotle: The Revised Oxford Translation*, vol. 2, ed. Jonathan Barnes (Princeton, N.J.: Princeton University Press, 1984), 1605 (§1016b).

6. Jacques Lacan, "Seminar on 'The Purloined Letter,'" in *Écrits*, 16.

7. Derrida, *Post Card*, 488. [The English translation omits the word *atomystic* entirely.—Trans.]

8. When Slavoj Žižek, in an attack, which is as rapid as it is summary, against what he calls "deconstructionism" (consisting, according to him, of "wrapping up commonsensical insights into an intricate jargon"), goes after "this Derridean reaction," he misses the essential point, precisely the punctiform character of the letter. See Žižek, *Enjoy Your Symptom! Jacques Lacan in Hollywood and Out* (New York: Routledge,

1992), 25n18; 9. Žižek doesn't say a word about this indivisibility of the Lacanian letter, occupied as he is with defending the idea that the letter "always arrives at its destination." Yet it is indeed *because it is indivisible* that the letter, as Derrida shows, "can circulate, intact." The real stakes in the Lacano-Derridean debate—which Žižek appears not to notice—are indeed the "atomystic." As Derrida writes, "It would be impossible to exaggerate the import of the proposition about the indivisibility of the letter, or rather about the letter's self-identity that is inaccessible to fragmentation" (*Post Card*, 466).

9. Lacan, *Seminar III*, 267.

10. See Nancy and Lacoue-Labarthe, *Title of the Letter*: "We quite simply substitute a cross-section of a bed, as it were, for the 'river' of the Saussurean schema of the 'floating kingdoms'" (54). (When he introduced his schema, Saussure in fact spoke of a "floating kingdom" to describe "thought . . . as a vague, uncharted nebula" while "phonic substance is neither more fixed nor more rigid than thought": It is therefore "language [*la langue*]" that, as "link between thought and sound," introduces into the one as into the other "reciprocal delimitations of units." Ferdinand de Saussure, *Course in General Linguistics*, trans. Wade Baskin, ed. Charles Bally and Albert Sechehaye [New York: Philosophical Library, 1959], 111–12).

11. The author here cites the translation of *Écrits* by Bruce Fink that is used throughout this translation, with the exception that, in order to maintain the play on the word *point*, "point de capiton" is rendered as "button point."—Trans. See also Bruce Fink's excellent commentary, *Lacan to the Letter: Reading Écrits Closely* (Minneapolis: University of Minnesota Press, 2004), 89 and 113.

12. Jacques Lacan, *Le Séminaire*, V, *Les Formations de l'inconscient* (Paris: Seuil, 1998), 13: "The relation of the signifier to the signified, which is so tangible in this dramatic dialogue, has led me to refer to Ferdinand de Saussure's famous schema, where one sees represented the double, parallel waves of the signifier and the signified, which are distinct and destined to perpetual slippage, one on top of the other. It is in connection with this that I have formed for you the image, borrowed from upholstery, of the button point. At some point, the material of the one must be attached to the material of the other for us to know what to hold onto, at least at the possible limits of these slippages. There are thus button points, but they leave some elasticity in the connections between the two terms."

13. See Lacan, "Subversion of the Subject and the Dialectic of Desire."

14. *Trait d'union* can also be translated as *hyphen*.—Trans.

15. On the diastole and other marks of separation used in reading since antiquity, see Paul Saenger, *Space between Words: The Origins of Silent Reading* (Stanford, Calif.: Stanford University Press, 1997), 54ff.

6 / Phrasing, or The Holes in Meaning

1. "Response to Jean Hyppolite's Commentary on Freud's 'Verneinung,'" in *Écrits: The First Complete Edition in English*, trans. Bruce Fink (New York: Norton, 2002), 324.

2. Henri Michaux, *Les Grandes Épreuves de l'esprit et les innombrables petites* (1966), in *Oeuvres complètes* (Paris: Gallimard, 2004), 3:391; *The Major Ordeals of the Mind and the Countless Minor Ones*, trans. Richard Howard (New York: Helen and Kurt Wolff, 1974), 117.

3. Henri Michaux, "La mescaline et la musique," in *Connaissance par les gouffres* (*Oeuvres complètes* [Paris: Gallimard, 2004]), 3:37); "Mescaline and Music," in *Light*

through Darkness, trans. Haakon Chevalier (New York: Orion Press, 1963), 49; the note is found on 208–9. [Translations are sometimes lightly modified.—Trans.] It would be impossible not to pay homage here to Philippe Lacoue-Labarthe's book *Phrase* (Paris: Christian Bourgois, 2000), as well as to the great little text by Rodolphe Burger, "Sur Ornette Coleman" (*Détail* 3/4 [1991]), from which I take the following: "What are we to understand by 'it phrases' when dealing with a musical statement? 'It speaks' or 'it sings' are poor equivalents. They say too much (it speaks but it says nothing; this is no way to speak; it sings but it is not simply a melodic statement)" (52).

4. Henri Michaux, "*Cannabis indica*," in *Connaissance par les gouffres*, 75–76; "Cannabis Indica," in *Light through Darkness*, 102–3.

5. These "arrests of a grave character," moreover, pose a problem for Michaux: "There were also passages with three dashes, but I surely let a good many pass without noting them. How to note an absence when you yourself are absent? But I had to, I knew that I had to circumscribe it, bring it to consciousness, with my consciousness in shreds take the measure of my unconsciousness. I could, I believe, with less difficulty, have knocked on the table, which a person (if such a one had been present) could have noted, as well as the duration of the attack. The small 'dot-holes' had been only at the beginning. The absence-holes now were but slices of absence. Many slices of absence" (ibid., 121–22; translation modified).

6. "There is no element in which language resembles music more than in the punctuation marks. The comma and the period correspond to the half-cadence and the authentic cadence. Exclamation marks are like the silent cymbal clashes, question marks like musical upbeats, colons dominant seventh chords." Theodor Adorno, "Punctuation Marks," in *Notes to Literature*, volume 2, ed. Rolf Tiedemann, trans. Shierry Weber Nicholsen (New York: Columbia University Press, 1991), 92.

7. Friedrich Nietzsche, *The Birth of Tragedy and The Case of Wagner*, trans. Walter Kaufmann (New York: Vintage Books, 1966), 178–79 (§11).

8. Hugo Riemann and Carl Fuchs, *Katechismus der Phrasierung* (Leipzig: Max Hesse Verlag, 1890).

9. Friedrich Nietzsche, *Sämtliche Briefe* (Frankfurt: Deutscher Taschenbuch Verlag / Walter de Gruyter, 2003), 8:401; *Selected Letters of Friedrich Nietzsche*, ed. and trans. Christopher Middleton (Indianapolis: Hackett, 1996), 306. [The translation is modified, sometimes fairly significantly, with an ear to the author's French translation.—Trans.] In the medieval and classical rhetorical treatises, the *colon* designated a major division of the period (hence: a medium punctuation); and the *comma* a subdivision of the *colon* (hence: a weak punctuation). Saint Jerome, in his translation of the Bible, generalized the so-called *per cola et commata* layout, that is, returning to the left margin for each new division or subdivision of the period (see Malcolm Parkes, *Pause and Effect: An Introduction to the History of Punctuation in the West* [Berkeley: University of California Press, 1993], 15).

10. Friedrich Nietzsche, "Assorted Maxims and Opinions," in *Human All Too Human*, trans. R. J. Hollingdale (Cambridge: Cambridge University Press, 1996), 244 (§134).

11. Friedrich Nietzsche, *Dawn: Thoughts on the Presumptions of Morality*, trans. Brittain Smith, vol. 5 of *The Complete Works of Friedrich Nietzsche*, ed. Alan D. Schrift, Keith Ansell-Pearson, and Duncan Large (Stanford, Calif.: Stanford University Press, 2011), §255.

12. It would be necessary here to reread in detail the passages from the seminar *Les Psychoses* (*Seminar III: The Psychoses*, trans. Russell Grigg, ed. Jacques-Alain Miller

[New York: Norton, 1993]), especially page 299, where Lacan speaks about the second person singular—"tu" [informal "you"—Trans.]—not only as a sort of "otolith" like those little stones present in the inner ear, but also and especially as a "hooking-up" or a "hooking of the other in the waters of meaning." He then writes, "This term that is used to identify the other at a point in these waters is a form of punctuation." Or again, "The *you* is a signifier, a punctuation by which the other is secured at a point of meaning." As for the triangulation of the structure of address of listening, it is quite precisely what I described in *Écoute, une histoire de nos oreilles* (Paris: Minuit, 2001), *Listen: A History of Our Ears*, trans. Charlotte Mandell (New York: Fordham University Press, 2008).

13. If one wished to find antecedents of Tyler, one might think of those amazing "flappers" [in French, "frappeurs," also "hitters"—Trans.] Jonathan Swift describes when Gulliver arrives at the flying island of Laputa: servants who "now and then flapped [*frappaient*] the Mouths and Ears" of their masters, who could neither "speak, or attend to the Discourses of others, without being roused by some external Taction." *Gulliver's Travels*, in *The Writings of Jonathan Swift*, ed. Robert A. Greenberg and William B. Piper (New York: Norton, 1973), 132.

14. The French pronoun *il* (*er*, in German) could be a person or a thing, a *he* or an *it*. See note 15 below.—Trans.

15. One will note that *il* [he or it] appears when B says to A: "Pull up close to me!" that is, when one of the angles in the triangulation closes, A and B almost merge into a single listener who is "all ears." Entirely attuned to what is being played, without anyone else coming to distract him. And it is then that, as a result, *il* makes his or its appearance *in the music*, as though the flattening of listening onto a straight line left the field open to the auctorial instance, thus giving birth, by projection, to what, in *Listen*, I called "total" or "structural" listening.

7 / The Dotted Lines of Auscultation

1. René Théophile Hyacinthe Laënnec, *De l'auscultation mediate ou Traité du diagnostic des maladies des poumons et du Coeur, fondé principalement sur ce nouveau moyen d'exploration* (Paris: J.-A. Brosson and J.-S. Chaudé Libraries, 1819).

2. Friedrich Nietzsche, *Twilight of the Idols; or, How to Philosophize with the Hammer*, trans. Richard Polt (Indianapolis: Hackett, 1997), 3. [The translation of Nietzsche's text is modified to follow more closely the author's French translation, which renders *aushorchen*—usually translated as "to sound out"—as *ausculter*, to auscultate, with its more technical medical sense. It is worth nothing that the Grimm brothers' dictionary glosses *aushorchen* as *auscultando explorare*. —Trans.]

3. A strange oscillation this, between the subject and the object of punctuation: The question mark in the end questions the one who poses it, and who should in turn relieve himself of it, cure himself of it by engaging in a punctuating and questioning auscultation of the idols. This back-and-forth, this mad exchange between the punctuating subject and the punctuated object, we have already recognized in Perekladin's "case."

4. Laënnec, *De l'auscultation mediate*, xxx–xxxi and 4. In Corvisart's 1808 translation, Auenbrugger's work (*Inventum novum ex percussione thoracis humani ut signo abstrusos interni pectoris morbos detegendi*) is titled *Nouvelle Méthode pour reconnaître les maladies internes de la poitrine par la percussion de cette cavité* (*New Method for Identifying Internal Chest Diseases by Means of the Percussion of the Cavity*)—I cite

the republication that appeared in Paris from Adolphe Delahays, Librarian, in 1855, as an appendix to Corvisart's *Essai sur les maladies et les lesions organiques du coeur et des gros vaisseaux* (*Essay on the Organic Diseases and Lesions of the Heart and Great Vessels*). Auenbrugger is also the author of an opera booklet for the composer Antonio Salieri: *Der Rauchfangkehrer*, produced on 30 April 1781.

5. John Forbes, *Original Cases with Dissections and Observations Illustrating the use of the Stethoscope and Percussion in the Diagnosis of Diseases of the Chest; Also Commentaries on the Same Subjects selected and translated from Auenbrugger, Corvisart, Laennec* (London, 1824), 5.

6. In *Listen: A History of Our Ears*, trans. Charlotte Mandell (New York: Fordham University Press, 2008), 134–36, I emphasized the importance of such a *digital* figure of listening in recent musical developments and equipment. But, following Jacques Derrida in *On Touching—Jean-Luc Nancy*, trans. Christine Irizarry (Stanford, Calif.: Stanford University Press, 2005), it would also have to be reinscribed at the heart of a whole philosophical tradition that passes, in particular, through Maine de Biran (*Influence de l'habitude sur la faculté de penser*, 1803) and his attempt to "relate hearing to touch," to "make hearing, listening, and the voice kinds of touching, modulations of haptic reconciliation or appropriation" (171).

7. René Théophile Hyacinthe Laënnec, *A Treatise on the Treatment of the Chest and on Mediate Auscultation*, trans. J. Forbes (London: Longman, 1834). [The translation is often quite loose and does not follow the French consistently, omitting numerous passages. When citing—often with modifications—the text parenthetically, I have marked the French text "F" and the translation "E."—Trans.]

8. The word *stethoscope* is odd, if we think about it, since it remains connected to the sight (*skopos*) of the one who observes, and even to the action of spying on (*skopia*) the chest (*stēthos*) as the seat of breathing, the voice, the heart. Moreover, Laënnec seems to have hesitated a bit: "I never believed it necessary to give a name to such a simple instrument; others have judged differently, and I have heard it called different names, all improper and sometimes barbarous, among others *sonometer*, *pectoriloc*, *thoraciloc*, *medical cornet*, etc. If one wants to give it a name, the one that would fit best is *stethoscope*."

9. See Michel Foucault, *The Birth of the Clinic: An Archaeology of Medical Perception*, trans. A. M. Sheridan (New York: Routledge, 1973): "The sign . . . assumes shape and value only within the questions posed by medical investigation. There is nothing, therefore, to prevent it being solicited and almost fabricated by medical investigation. . . . This explains why Corvisart was able, without any major theoretical problem, to reactivate Auenbrugger's relatively old and completely forgotten discovery. . . . It was natural that clinical medicine at the end of the eighteenth century should ignore a technique that made a sign appear artificially where there had been no symptom, and solicited a response when the disease itself did not speak. . . . But as soon as pathological anatomy compels the clinic to question the body in its organic density, and to bring to the surface what was given only in deep layers, the idea of a technical artifice capable of surprising a lesion becomes once again a scientifically based idea. The return to Auenbrugger can be explained. . . . Sounding by percussion is not justified if the disease is composed only of a web of symptoms; it becomes necessary if the patient is hardly more than an injected corpse, a half-filled barrel" (162).

10. Ibid., 166, my emphasis. Certain hurried readers of Foucault have found in his comments an impenitent oculocentrism, in particular when he writes: "The medical

gaze is now endowed with a plurisensorial structure. A gaze that touches, hears, and, moreover, not by essence or necessity, sees. . . . The sensorial triangulation indispensable to anatomo-clinical perception remains under the dominant sign of the visible: first, because this multi-sensorial perception is merely a way of anticipating the triumph of the gaze that is represented by the autopsy; and ear and hand are merely temporary, substitute organs until such time as death brings to truth the luminous presence of the visible; it is a question of a mapping in life, that is, in night, in order to indicate how things would be in the white brightness of death. And above all, the alterations discovered by anatomy concern . . . spatial data that belong by right of origin to the gaze. . . . When Corvisart hears a heart that functions badly or Laënnec a voice that trembles, what they see with that gaze that secretly haunts their hearing and, beyond it, animates it, is a hypertrophy, a discharge" (164–65). Jonathan Sterne goes so far as to attribute to Foucault "an essentially theological argument about the origins and purposes of the senses" (*The Audible Past* [Durham, N.C.: Duke University Press, 2003], 127). You have to rub your eyes and wonder what in the world the author was reading. For as Foucault himself says explicitly, the look he is speaking about is that of the "absolute visibility" of the "absolute eye of knowledge" (166, translation modified slightly). It is this look—that of the *idea*, if you will—that is sovereign, that imposes the "sovereignty of the visible" (166). Far from a shameless oculocentrism, Foucault knows that one cannot with a single gesture sweep away the entire weight of plurimillenarian history that makes of vision the touchstone of knowledge, in Laënnec as elsewhere.

11. Raymond Queneau, *Zazie in the Metro*, trans. Barbara Wright (London: John Calder Press, 1982): "While they waited for the livid-fleshed waitress to withdraw so that at last some words of love might blossom through the bulbulating of their beers" (138).

8 / Monauralisms, or The Bubble of Quotation Marks

The French title, "Monoreilles," combines the prefix indicating the singular, *mono-*, or the first person singular possessive pronoun, *mon*, with the plural *oreilles*, ears. A literal translation would give something like *monoears*.—Trans.

1. Jacques Derrida, "Tympan," in *Margins of Philosophy*, trans. Alan Bass (Chicago: University of Chicago Press, 1982), x and xii.

2. Friedrich Nietzsche, *Twilight of the Idols; or, How to Philosophize with the Hammer*, trans. Richard Polt (Indianapolis: Hackett, 1997), 3.

3. The most immediate meanings of *feuille* are similar to those of the English *leaf*.—Trans.

4. Jacques Derrida, *Of Grammatology*, trans. Gayatri Chakravorty Spivak (Baltimore: Johns Hopkins University Press, 1974), 227. He continues: "Accents are, like punctuation, an evil of writing: not only an invention of *copyists* but of copyists who are *strangers* to the language which they transcribe" (227). While Nietzsche noted that "the art of writing requires above all *substitutes* for the modes of expression that only a speaking subject has available: hence for gestures, accents, tones, looks." See §110 of *The Wanderer and His Shadow* in *Human, All Too Human II and Unpublished Fragments*, trans. Gary Handwerk (Stanford, Calif.: Stanford University Press, 2013), 203.

5. Jacques Derrida, *Of Spirit: Heidegger and the Question*, trans. Geoffrey Bennington and Rachel Bowlby (Chicago: University of Chicago Press, 1989), 25. In *Signéponge = Signsponge*, trans. Richard Rand (New York: Columbia University Press,

1984), Derrida describes quotation marks as "tweezers" (44) or "clothespins" to "put [a sentence] out to dry" "as photographers now and then do to develop a print" (2, translation modified).

6. "Quotation marks are not heard or are heard everywhere," Derrida writes in *Parages*, trans. Tom Conley, James Hulbert, John P. Leavey, and Avital Ronell (Stanford, Calif.: Stanford University Press, 2011), 40.

7. Marcel Proust, *Swann's Way: In Search of Lost Time*, ed. William C. Carter, trans. C. K. Scott Moncrieff (New Haven, Conn.: Yale University Press, 2013), 111: "As [Swann] spoke I noticed, what had often struck me before in his conversations with my grandmother's sisters, that whenever he spoke of serious matters, whenever he used an expression which seemed to imply a definite opinion on some important subject, he would take care to isolate it by using a special intonation, mechanical and ironic, as though he had put the phrase or word in quotation marks, and was anxious to disclaim any personal responsibility for it" (96). On invisible quotation marks in Derrida, see especially *Of Spirit: Heidegger and the Question*: "look at Valéry's invisible quotation marks" (123), and "Heidegger here inscribes invisible quotation marks" (95), as well as "Living On," in *Parages*, ed. John P. Leavey, trans. James Hulbert (Stanford, Calif.: Stanford University Press, 2011): "We have to glimpse or overhear quotation marks," and "these invisible quotation marks remain invisible" (104, translation modified).

8. Friedrich Nietzsche, *Nachlaß 1884–1885*, volume 11 of the *Kritische Studienausgabe*, ed. Giorgio Colli and Mazzino Montinari (Berlin: Deutscher Taschenbuch Verlag, 1999), 580. [The translation follows as closely as possible the French translation given by the author.—Trans.]

9. Jacques Derrida, "On a Newly Arisen Apocalyptic Tone in Philosophy," in *Raising the Tone of Philosophy: Late Essays by Immanuel Kant, Transformative Critique by Jacques Derrida*, ed. Peter Fenves, trans. John Leavey Jr. (Baltimore: John Hopkins University Press, 1993), 123.

10. Martin Heidegger, *The Principle of Reason*, trans. Reginald Lilly (Bloomington: Indiana University Press, 1991), 39–40.

11. Jacques Derrida, *Politics of Friendship*, trans. George Collin (London: Verso, 1999), 189. [Translations sometimes modified.—Trans.]

12. Jacques Derrida, "Heidegger's Ear: Philopolemology (*Geschlecht* IV)," trans. John P. Leavey Jr., in *Reading Heidegger: Commemorations*, ed. John Sallis (Bloomington: Indiana University Press, 1993), 215. [The essay was published in French as the concluding chapter of *Politics of Friendship*. It is not included in the English edition.—Trans.]

13. See especially Jacques Derrida, "Restitutions of the Truth in Pointing [*pointure*]," in *The Truth in Painting*, by Jacques Derrida, trans. Geoff Bennington and Ian McLeod (Chicago: University of Chicago Press, 1987), where Derrida, repeating Heidegger's quotation of Knut Hamsun in *Introduction to Metaphysics* ("The poet says: 'He is seated here between his ears and he hears the veritable void'"), writes: "He speaks of two ears, of a pair of ears perhaps, apparently undetachable, but whose *being-double* permits the stereophony of the void to let itself be heard" (379).

14. See Derrida, "Heidegger's Ear": "The animal that is 'poor in world,' that has neither language nor experience of death, etc., the animal that has no hand, the animal that has no friend, has no ear either, the ear . . . that opens Dasein to its own potentiality-for-being and that, as we will hear in a moment, is the ear of being, the ear for being." And further down: "The animal, if something like that existed that had some unity, would have no ear. No ear capable of hearing" (172; translation sometimes lightly modified).

15. The second part of this sentence (after "prehensile organs") is not found in the English translation: "Heidegger's Ear: Philopolemology (*Geschlecht* IV)." [The first sentence is taken from the English translation. The French differs from that point, and the remainder of the passage is my translation.—Trans.]

16. Jonathan Sterne, *The Audible Past: Cultural Origins of Sound Reproduction* (Durham, N.C.: Duke University Press, 2003), 156. The article is by Dr. George Carrick, "On the Differential Stethoscope and Its Value in the Discrimination of Diseases of the Lungs and Heart," *Aberdeen Medical and Chirurgical Tracts* 12, no. 9 (1873): 902.

17. The French *topologie* and the neologism *taupologie* are homophones. *Taupologie* is derived from *taupe*, mole.—Trans.

18. Martin Heidegger, "European Nihilism," in *Nietzsche* II. In the preface to *Dawn: Thoughts on the Presumptions of Morality*, trans. Brittain Smith (Stanford, Calif.: Stanford University Press, 2011), Nietzsche depicts himself as a "mole" (*Maulwurf*), a "'subterranean' at work, a tunneler, miner, underminer" (1) [*einen "Unterirdischen" an der Arbeit, einen Bohrenden, Grabenden, Untergrabenden*]. See *All Ears: The Aesthetics of Espionage*, trans. Roland Végső (New York: Fordham University Press, 2017), where I explore different topmological [*taupologique*] figures of hearing, recalling also that the archaic French noun *écoute* [a listener] could indicate, for instance, "a guard stationed in a mining tunnel charged with monitoring the progression, the development of the enemy miner's work," or even "a miner himself, stationed as sentinel" (51; see also 52–58).

19. At the beginning of the eighth session of *The Principle of Reason*, Heidegger writes thus: "*Sein und Grund: das Selbe*, 'being and ground/reason: the same'" (Heidegger, *Principle of Reason*, 59). Heidegger also listens attentively to the different values of the colon [*Doppelpunkt*] in the texts and lectures that constitute *On the Way to Language*: At times colons announce who or what is going to speak ("What follows speaks, seen grammatically, in the indicative" [141]), at times they gather together or collect in advance ("a colon that includes everything that follows" [194]), as though in order for them better to reopen what they have taken in thus ("this colon must make heard that what precedes it opens into what follows it" [94]). *On the Way to Language*, trans. Peter D. Hertz (New York: Harper & Row, 1971) [translations modified—Trans].

20. See Jacques Derrida, *Monolingualism of the Other*, trans. Patrick Mensah (Stanford, Calif.: Stanford University Press, 1998), where in recounting a dialogue with the Moroccan sociologist and writer Abdelkebir Khatibi, Derrida writes that he "holds the voluble conch of a double language against his ear" (36).

9 / *Punctum Saliens*, or The Salient Point

1. G. W. F. Hegel, *Phenomenology of Spirit*, trans. A. V. Miller (Oxford: Oxford University Press, 1977), 64.

2. To put this in more rigorously Hegelian terms, nature, considered as the idea's exit from itself (as its becoming-other [§247]), is initially pure and simple exteriority, undifferentiated: "The first or immediate determination of Nature is *Space*: the abstract *universality of Nature's self-externality* [*die abstrakte* Allgemeinheit ihres Aussersichseins], self-externality's mediationless indifference [*dessen vermittlungslose Gleichgültigkeit*, der Raum]" (§254). Hegel, *Philosophy of Nature*, trans. A. V. Miller (Oxford: Oxford University Press, 1970), 28. See also the addendum to §254: "the Heres are side by side and do not interfere with each other [*die Hier sind eins neben dem andern*,

ohne sich zu stören]. . . . The Heres are also different; but the difference is equally no difference, i.e. it is an abstract difference [*die Hier sind auch unterschieden; aber der Unterschied ist ebenso kein Unterschied, d.h. es ist der abstrakte Unterschied*]. Space is therefore punctiformity [*der Raum ist also Punktualität*], but a negative punctiformity [*die aber eine nichtige ist*], and so perfect continuity [*volkommene Kontinuität*]" (29).

3. G. W. F. Hegel, *Jenaer Systementwurf III* (1805–6). Cited by Markus Semm in his beautiful essay, *Der springende Punkt in Hegels System* (Berlin: Boer, 1994), 85. I thank my friend Thomas Schestag for putting me on the path of the punctuating pulsations in the Hegelian corpus.

4. William Harvey, "Anatomical Exercises on the Generation of Animals," in *The Works of William Harvey*, trans. Robert Willis (London: C. and J. Ablard, 1848), 235–36.

5. One would need to question at length the place, the strange status, of the plant in the *Philosophy of Nature*. For what it contains are the seeds, if I dare put it thus, of an entire discourse on *grafting*. Thus, when Hegel writes (in the addendum to §337) that "each plant is . . . an infinite number of subjects" and especially when he speaks, later, of what he calls the "universal vegetation" (*allgemeine Vegetation*) of lichens or moss (addendum to §341), the distinction between the organic and the inorganic is not far from flying into pieces: "Such are lichen, *moss*, into which every stone breaks forth [*das sind die Flechten, das* Moos, *worin jeder Stein ausschlägt*]. . . . This vegetation, as not yet shaped by individuality (*als noch nicht Bildung der Individualität*), consists of inorganic-organic forms [*unorganisch-organische Gebilde*] like lichens and fungi which one does not rightly know how to classify [*von denen man nicht recht weiss, was man daraus machen soll*]" (298). Has a stone ever been known to produce buds? ["Buds" are here *bourgeons*, and the French translation of *ausschlägt*, rendering the stones that "break forth" above, is "bourgeonne"—Trans.] And what are we to do with the inorganic-organic? Where to put it? Let us simply remark here that Hegel's text itself, and even every text in general, could be described as a plant, more precisely a lichen or moss. Organic-inorganic, the text lends itself exemplarily to grafting.

6. Hegel, *Philosophy of Nature*, §359. I prefer, for reasons that should now be more readily apparent, to translate *springende Punkt* as "pulsating point" rather than as "point saillant [salient point]," as Bernard Bourgeois and Augusto Vera propose. [I have followed the author's French translation, where the English has "*punctum saliens* of selfhood."—Trans.]

10 / The Point of the Overcast Stitch

1. See also in G. W. F. Hegel, *Philosophy of Nature*, trans. A. V. Miller (Oxford: Oxford University Press, 1970), the brief §311: "On the one hand the extreme of the *punctiform principle*, of brittleness, and on the other hand the extreme of fluidity assuming a *spherical* shape [*einerseits das Extrem* der Punktualität *der Sprödigkeit, andererseits das Extrem der sich* kugelnden *Flüssigkeit*]." See also the addendum to this same paragraph: "The determinations of form . . . are first the point, then the line and surface, and lastly the total volume. The brittle [*das Spröde*] body is pulverizable [*das Pulvrige*], . . . granular [*das Körnige*]" (162).

2. Hegel, *Philosophy of Nature*, §300: "im Erzittern, *d. i. durch die momentane ebenso Negation der Teile wie Negation dieser ihrer Negation, die aneinander gebunden eine durch die andere erweckt wird, und so, als ein Oszillieren des Bestehens und*

der Negation der spezifischen Schwere und Kohäsion, . . . kommt als diese mechanische Seelenhaftigkeit zur Erscheinung."

3. See Hegel, *Philosophy of Nature*, the addendum to §351: "Sound belongs to the animal in such a manner that it is the animal's own activity that makes the bodily organism vibrate" (354–55). And a few lines above this: "The inorganic does not show its specific quality until it is stimulated from outside, gets struck [*angeschlagen*]; but the animal sounds of its own accord" (354).

4. See the second chapter of the first part, titled "Natural Beauty."

5. In *Prophecies of Leviathan: Reading Past Melville*, trans. Gil Anidjar (New York: Fordham University Press, 2010), I named this a "contraction of the self, accompanied by a panoramic expansion" (58). Discontraction, the systole-diastole, and the *punctum saliens* are clearly possible faces of negation and of the negation of negation—of the point that is (not) a point. [Here and in the main text, the author plays on two meanings of the French *point*: as dot, point, period, and as negative particle, like *pas*.—Trans.]

6. G. W. F. Hegel, *Aesthetics: Lectures on Fine Art*, trans. T. M. Knox (Oxford: Clarendon Press, 1975), 1:153–54.

7. See the article "Cloth (workers in)" in Diderot and D'Alembert's *Encyclopédie*: "The different sewing stitches are the *surget*, which pulls the cloths together by the edges . . . ." The *Littré*, for its part, under the entry "surjet" offers: "1. A stitch used to bring solidly together two edges or pieces of material folded in a straight line or at an angle; it is made by stitching with the needle at once a bit of the edge of the two borders placed one on top of the other or of the two pieces of fabric brought together exactly one on top of the other and tightening the stitches . . . 2. Term from book-binding. A kind of sewing done to books." Jacques Derrida alludes to the overcast stitch as it is also used for surgical grafts in *Dissemination*, trans. Barbara Johnson (Chicago: University of Chicago Press, 1981), 355.

8. See Markus Semm, *Der springende Punkt in Hegels System* (Berlin: Boer, 1994), 136 and 145.

9. As Alexandre Koyré rightly emphasizes, "Hegel's thought . . . moves in leaps" ("Hegel à Jena" [1934], in *Études d'histoire de la pensée philosophique* [Paris: Gallimard, 1990], 148). It is thus perhaps as *jolts* that we should understand the pulsations that animate "simple infinity or the absolute concept" (*diese einfache Unendlichkeit oder der absolute Begriff*): Hegel himself describes them as "universal blood, whose omnipresence is neither disturbed nor interrupted by any difference, but rather is itself every difference, as also their supersession; it pulsates within itself but does not move, inwardly vibrates, yet is at rest." Hegel, *Phenomenology of Spirit*, trans. A. V. Miller (Oxford: Oxford University Press, 1977), 100.

10. Gérard Genette, *Figures III* (Paris: Le Seuil, 1972), 75.

11. We would have to question, here, what Markus Semm (*Der springende Punkt*, 136–37) names "vocalization" (*Vokalisation*). For the voice in question is a voice that is strictly *internal* to the system: It is even, quite simply, the voice that this system produces or constructs. Now, there again we should distinguish between an intra- and a metadiegetic voice, since everything at stake in the reading voice is situated *between the two*. Let us note in passing that Hegel on the whole speaks quite little of the voice as such in his *Lectures on Fine Art*. Most of all, there are scattered allusions: to the "free-sounding of the animal voice" (1:122), vocal freedom no longer being limited

here, it seems, to birds alone, as in the *Philosophy of Nature*; and to the "human voice," which, contrary to that of the colossal statues of Memnon, "resonates from inside" without need of any "external impulse" (1:358); to the same colossuses (2:41); to the "pure voices" of "Italian music" (301); to "vocal music" inasmuch as it "also articulates words"; and there is a passing consideration of "the sound of the voice and the mode of recitation" in declamation (653). Nonetheless, there are two brief passages that deserve to be read more closely for our purposes. The first, which is found in the chapter on music, compares the human voice to human skin, to that epidermis on whose surface the *punctum saliens* shows. "Just as we saw [in the chapter on painting, 2:846], in the case of the colour of the human skin, that, as an ideal unity, it contains the rest of the colours and therefore is the most perfect colour, so the human voice contains the ideal totality of sound [*des Klingens*], a totality only spread out amongst the other instruments in their particular differences. Consequently, it is the perfection of sound [*das vollkommene Tönen*]" (922). But this perfection of voice is such only if it is unmixed, that is, when it has perfectly absorbed or melted in itself all of its components: "Voice must above all," Hegel writes, "be pure, i.e. along with the perfect note no noise [*Geräusch*] of any kind should assert itself" (922). And what, then, is the purity of voice? It is at bottom, Hegel explains in the second passage that is of interest to us, its distinctly *vocalic* character, that is, the distinction of its *vowels*; thus, he notes, in the chapter on natural beauty: "The pure sound of the voice [*der reine Klang der Stimme*], merely as a pure note [*als blosser reiner Ton*], is infinitely pleasing and impressive. . . . In a similar way speech too has pure notes like the vowels a, e, i, o, u, and mixed notes like ä, ü, ö. Popular dialects especially have impure sounds [*unreine Klänge*], mediants like *oa*. A further point about the purity of notes [*die Reinheit der Vokalklänge*] is that the vowels should be associated with such consonants as do not blur the purity of the vowel sounds. The northern languages frequently weaken the vowel sounds with their consonants, whereas Italian preserves the purity of the vowel sounds and for that reason is so singable [*sangbar*]" (142). Consonants are thus like the percussions of language, since they cannot be sung (to see, try vocalizing on a *t* or a *k*). They are the interruption of song, the punctuation of vocal melody. Or, inversely, melody as *vocalic line* is the sublation of percussive punctiformity: In the chapter on music, Hegel speaks of percussion instruments "struck at one point" (*das punktuelle Anschlagen*) whose sublation (*Sichaufheben*) is the "direction of a line" (*die lineare Richtung*) (2:921).

11 / Ekphrasis

1. It appeared in *Studio International* 180, no. 924 (1970): 38. Erica DiBenedetto drew my attention to this beautiful page; I thank her here, as well as the other students in my seminar at Princeton University in 2012: Victoria Aschheim, Harriet Calver, Joppan George, Jesse McCarthy, Federica Soletta, and Ashmi Thapar.

2. This is really its modern definition, for the ancient conception of ekphrasis in no way reduced it to a description applied exclusively to translating images in the sense in which we understand it. See Ruth Webb, *Ekphrasis, Imagination and Persuasion in Ancient Rhetorical Theory and Practice* (London: Ashgate, 2009).

3. Franz Kafka, *The Trial*, trans. Mike Mitchell (Oxford: Oxford University Press, 2009). Translations are sometimes modified slightly. It is well known that the posthumous editions of *The Trial*, beginning with the one published by Max Brod in 1925, have each organized the sequence of chapters differently. Nevertheless, most agree that

"Lawyer, Manufacturer, Painter" be placed before the chapter with the parable, "In the Cathedral."

4. There is, of course, the "dark portrait" of a man with his head "bent so low" described briefly in the first chapter of *The Castle*, as well as other "photos" picked out by Deleuze and Guattari in *Kafka: Toward a Minor Literature*, trans. Dana Polan (Minneapolis: University of Minnesota Press, 1986), 3.

5. The French *surimpression* also designates double exposure.—Trans.

6. *The Trial: A Film by Orson Welles*, English translation and description of action by Nicholas Fry (New York: Simon and Schuster, 1970), 156.

7. As the next chapter details, *bonimenter* is not only chatter but the technical term for film explaining that accompanied early, "silent" films.—Trans.

8. See Barbara Cassin's excellent article, "'Ekphrasis': From Word to Word," in *Dictionary of Untranslatables: A Philosophical Lexicon*, edited by Barbara Cassin, Emily Apter, Jacques Lezra, and Michael Wood (Princeton, NJ: Princeton University Press, 2014), 205. On ekphrastic logic in general, see also W. J. T. Mitchell, "Ekphrasis and the Other," in *Picture Theory: Essays on Verbal and Visual Representation* (Chicago: University of Chicago Press, 1994), 151–81. The Ovidian ekphrasis that we are preparing to read is not mentioned by Mitchell; it might, however, have led him, as we will see, to interrogate certain of his affirmations, for example, this one: "Unlike the encounters of verbal and visual representation in 'mixed arts' . . . the ekphrastic encounter in language is purely figurative. The image . . . cannot literally come into view. . . . The genre of ekphrasis . . . means that the textual other must remain completely alien" (157–58). By placing the emphasis on this radical alterity of image and text, does Mitchell not give in to what he himself calls the "ekphrastic fear" of their possible co-implication?

9. "Extended descriptions" here translates *descriptions filées*, which resonates with an extended metaphor, with the *fil* of *filées* picking up on the thread being woven throughout the discussion.—Trans.

10. The two successive ekphrases—of Minerva's work, and of Arachne's cloth— moreover, echo each other in their respective conclusions: Arachne's ivy responds to the "olive wreaths" with which Minerva completes her woven image, finishing her work with "emblems of her own tree" (line 102; the olive tree was the emblem of the Greek Pallas Athena).

11. Longus, *Daphnis and Chloe*, trans. Jeffrey Henderson (Cambridge, Mass.: Harvard University Press, 2009), 13.

12. This is no doubt what Barbara Cassin alludes to as well when, without explicitly mentioning this exegete, she nevertheless suggests that the entire romance is "the *ekphrasis* of an *ekphrasis*," a sort of copy of a copy (205).

13. Philippe Lacoue-Labarthe, *La Vraie Semblance* (Paris: Galilée, 2008): "It is *ekphrasis* itself (*de-scription*)" (79). Citing Lacoue-Labarthe's words in the framework of a study of the singular de-scriptive practice of Jean-Luc Nancy, Ginette Michaud similarly suggests that ekphrastic writing always aims, in a work, at an "exposition" of "what is not yet a work," of what remains, rather, a process, "always coming from or being formed through it." See "*Ek-phraseis* de Nancy," *Europe* 960 (April 2009). *Ekphrasis* as de-scription, I would say, is thus a sort of *unworking* of the work. One that passes through Ovid's intertexture more than through Longus's contragraphics. When Jean-Luc Nancy speaks of *ekphrasis* in "Distinct Oscillation," he takes the ekphrastic interlacing of image and text as far as it can go: "Each is the *ekphrasis* of the other." See *The Ground of the Image*, trans. Jeff Fort (New York: Fordham University Press, 2005), 75.

12 / General Chatter

The French title for this chapter is "Le Boniment Général." "Chatter" here translates *boniment* and is also implied in the related word *bonimenteur*, translated throughout in its specifically film historical sense of "film explainer."—Trans.

1. Jacques Lacan, *Four Fundamental Concepts of Psychoanalysis: Seminar Book XI*, trans. Alan Sheridan, ed. Jacques-Alain Miller (New York: W. W. Norton, 1998), 105.

2. *The Trial: A Film by Orson Welles*, English translation and description of action by Nicholas Fry (New York: Simon and Schuster, 1970), 158.

3. See Hanns Zischler, *Kafka Goes to the Movies*, trans. Susan H. Gillespie (Chicago: University of Chicago Press, 2002).

4. Germain Lacasse, *Le Bonimenteur de vues animées: Le Cinéma "muet" entre tradition et modernité* (Montreal: Nota Bene / Méridiens Klincksieck, 2000), 30.

5. Gert Hofmann, *The Film Explainer*, trans. Michael Hofmann (Evanston, Ill.: Northwestern University Press, 1996), 15. The novel's dedication reads: "In memoriam Karl Hofmann, 1873–1944, film explainer."

6. Throughout the development of how the film explainer makes the image and film good for something, the author draws on the root *bon* (good) in both *bonimenteur*, film explainer, and *bon à*, to be good for.—Trans.

7. See Peter Szendy, *Listen: A History of Our Ears*, trans. Charlotte Mandell (New York: Fordham University Press, 2008), 112–13, as well as *All Ears: The Aesthetics of Espionage*, trans. Roland Végső (New York: Fordham University Press, 2016).

8. Lacasse, *Le Bonimenteur de vues animées*, 164–65. Today, however, the art of the film explainer is the object of renewed interest that is not merely historical: One thus finds editions of explained films (like those of Méliès, with explanations by André Dussollier, in the 2008 boxed set by Studio Canal and Fencher Productions), but we are also witnessing a real renaissance in the practice of film explaining in the so-called "neo-benshi" movement in California.

9. Thus integrated, the film explainer then appears, retrospectively, as a sort of belated equivalent, a distant descendant, of the admonisher in painting as Alberti describes him (*De pictura*, 2.42): "It seems opportune then that *in the historia* [my emphasis: *in the pictorial work itself*, then] there is someone who informs the spectators of the things that unfold; or invites with the hand to show; or threatens with severe face and turbid eyes not to approach there, as if he wishes that a similar story remain secret; or indicates a danger or another [attribute] over there to observe; or invites you with his own gestures to laugh together or cry in company. It is necessary, in the end, that also all [the occurrences] that those painted [characters] made with the spectators and with themselves, concur to realize and explain the *historia* [*E piacemi sia* nella storia *chi ammonisca e insegni a noi quello che ivi si facci, o chiami con la mano a vedere, o con viso cruccioso e con gli occhi turbati minacci che niuno verso loro vada, o dimostri qualche pericolo o cosa ivi meravigliosa, o te inviti a piangere con loro insieme o a ridere. E così qualunque cosa fra loro o teco facciano i dipinti, tutto appartenga a ornare o a insegnarti la storia*]." In *Leon Battista Alberti: On Painting*, ed. Rocco Sinisgalli (Cambridge: Cambridge University Press, 2011), 63. In their article "Fonctions et origines du bonimenteur du cinéma des premiers temps," André Gaudreault and Germain Lacasse suggest that "these two figures of transmission, the admonisher and the film explainer, fulfill similar functions of demonstrating and commenting"; and they also indicate that the admonisher inscribes himself in the tradition of the *festaiuolo*, "the master

of ceremonies whose verbal discourse accompanied the famous medieval *Mysteries*" (*Cinémas* 4, no. 1 [1993]): 138–39). Finally, with montage, that "very cinematographic way of injecting narrative into images that are demonstrative," the film explainer as narrative instance ends up being "sucked up into film" (144–45). More recently, Jean-Michel Durafour has analyzed different continuations and consequences of this internalization of the film explainer (whom he designates with the Japanese term *katsuben*, a portmanteau made from *benshi* and *katsudo shashin*, that is, "animated photographs"). Thus, he notes that "the function of the *katsuben* can also be seen to be 'incorporated' into the fictional world of film, disconnected from his physical (extra-filmic) person, notably in the form of the voice-over . . . or the interpretive role that devolves to one or more secondary characters" ("Sur quelques avatars envisageables du *katsuben* dans le cinema japonais des années 1930," *Cinémas* 20, no. 1 [2009]: 47). The "*katsuben*-object" would also count among these "filmic avatars of the *katsuben*." Thus, in Ozu's *Tokyo Twilight*, "the camera continues to frame the steaming teapot after the mother, who has just learned of her son's death, leaves the frame, for with this teapot it is the *mother's tears* that are glossed" (56).

10. We find other spoken credits in Welles, in *The Magnificent Ambersons* (1942) and *Othello* (1952), but also, already, in Marcel L'Herbier in *Le Mystère de la chambre jaune* (1930).

11. *Le Cinéma* (1962), with music by Michel Legrand: "Sur l'écran noir de mes nuits blanches, / Moi je me fais du cinéma / Sans pognon et sans caméra, / Bardot peut partir en vacances: / Ma vedette, c'est toujours toi. / . . . Sur l'écran de mes nuits blanches, / Où je me fais du cinéma, / Une fois, deux fois, dix fois, vingt fois, / Je recommence la séquence / Où tu me tombes dans les bras [On the blank screen of my sleepless nights / I make movies. / Without dough and without cameras, / Bardot can take a vacation: / You are always my star. / . . . On the blank screen of my sleepless nights, / Where I make movies, / Once, twice, ten, twenty times, / I replay the sequence / Where you fall into my arms]."

12. The author's phrase "pulls out all the stops" ("fait des pieds et des mains"— more literally "uses his feet and hands") plays on "hands and feet" later in the sentence.—Trans.

13. On the *this* of sense certainty at the beginning of his *Phenomenology of Spirit*, Hegel, we recall, wrote that it is "pointing out [that] shows itself" (*zeigt sich das Aufzeigen*). See *Phenomenology of Spirit*, trans. A. V. Miller (Oxford: Oxford University Press, 1977), 64. For his part, Louis Marin spoke of the "double dimension" of every system of representation: Considering it in its "transitive" or "transparent" dimension, one can say that "every representation *represents* something," whereas in its "reflexive" dimension, in its "opacity," it "*represents itself* representing something" (*Opacité de la peinture: Essais sur la représentation au Quattrocento* [Paris: Éditions Usher, 1989], 73). Alberti's admonisher, to whom the film explainer can be compared, is for Marin such a figure (or rather, "metafigure") of the "presentation of representation in painting." See Louis Marin, *De la représentation* (Paris: École des Hautes Études-Gallimard-Le Seuil, 1994), 321.

14. Jean-Luc Nancy, "The Image—the Distinct," in *The Ground of the Image*, trans. Jeff Fort (New York: Fordham University Press, 2005), 2–3.

15. The pin screen is a blank screen perforated with numerous holes in which black pins are inserted. When light is projected at an angle, the shadow from the pins that

are pulled out makes the screen black; those that are stuck in, on the contrary, produce white.

16. Nancy, *Ground of the Image*, 63–79.

17. *The Trial: A Film by Orson Welles*, 166.

18. Lacan, *Four Fundamental Concepts of Psychoanalysis*, 96.

13 / Punctuation and Politics, or The Dot above the i

1. Leon Trotsky, "The October Strike," in *1905*, trans. Anya Bostock (New York: Random House, 1971), 85.

2. *The Case of Wagner*, in *The Birth of Tragedy* and *The Case of Wagner*, trans. Walter Kaufmann (New York: Vintage 1967), 179, translation modified.

3. *Selected Letters of Friedrich Nietzsche*, ed. and trans. Christopher Middleton (Indianapolis: Hackett, 1996), 306.

4. Friedrich Nietzsche, *Nachlaß 1880–1882*, vol. 9 of *Kritische Studienausgabe*, ed. Giorgio Colli and Mazzino Montinari (Munich: Deutscher Taschenbuch Verlag, 1999), 73. [The passage is translated from the German, in view of the author's French translation.—Trans.] Kandinsky put it well in *Point and Line to Plane*, "the desert is a sea of sand made up entirely of points." See *Point and Line to Plane*, trans. Howard Dearstyne, ed. Hilla Rebay (New York: Dover, 1979), 39.

5. Edwin Abbott, *Flatland: A Romance of Many Dimensions* (London: Dover, 1952), 93–94.

6. G. W. F. Hegel, *Elements of the Philosophy of Right*, trans. H. B. Nisbet, ed. Allen W. Wood (Cambridge: Cambridge University Press, 1991), 322–23. In *Rogues*, Derrida similarly described the "moment proper" of sovereignty as "the stigmatic point of an indivisible instant." And he added, "A pure sovereignty is indivisible or it is not at all." Jacques Derrida, *Rogues: Two Essays on Reason*, trans. Pascale-Anne Brault and Michael Naas (Stanford, Calif.: Stanford University Press, 2005), 100–101.

7. We should reread carefully the magnificent pages that Daniel Arasse devotes to the narratives of the decapitation of Louis XVI in *La Guillotine et l'imaginaire de la terreur* (Paris: Flammarion, 1987): "The important thing here is to note that, in all the republican versions, royal discourse is taken to its limit or, more precisely, to the limit of one of its phrases. The royalists, on the contrary, choose to interrupt Louis' discourse: ellipses mark where the guillotine cuts off the king's speech, allowing the margin of something unsaid to develop its suggestions. . . . The difference might seem minor, but it is revealing: for the republicans, the guillotine intervenes after the completion of a speech that is judged adequate to the extent that it has revealed its author's betrayal" (112). I myself have emphasized the motif of decapitation as the dotting of the i, that is of the "I" as sovereign subject. See *Prophecies of Leviathan: Reading Past Melville*, trans. Gil Anidjar (New York: Fordham University Press, 2010).

8. George W. Bush, 3 October 2006. Cited by Peter Baker, "Stepping Up Attacks, Bush Calls Democrats 'Softer' on Terrorists," *Washington Post*, 4 October 2006.

9. See the article "Ponctuation," by the grammarian Nicolas Beauzée, in Diderot and D'Alembert's *Encyclopédie*: "It is said that General Fairfax, instead of simply signing the death sentence of the King of England, Charles I, contrived a way of exonerating himself, if necessary, from the odious part of this process, and that he took a detour that, if well understood, was but another crime. He wrote without *punctuation* below the sentence: *si omnes consentiunt ego non dissentio*, allowing him to interpret his

statement, depending on the circumstances, by *punctuating* it thus: *si omnes consentiunt; ego non; dissentio* [if all consent, I do not; I oppose], instead of *punctuating* it according to the natural meaning that immediately presents itself and that he surely wanted to imply at the time: *si omnes consentiunt, ego non dissentio* [if all consent, I do not oppose]." An allusion to this same episode is found in Antoine Rivarol, in a note in his *Discours sur l'universalité de la langue française* (1784); the universalizing glorification of the clarity of French here goes hand in hand with the implicit warning about the mortal dangers that punctuation can harbor: "It [French] is of all languages the only one whose genius is combined with integrity. Certain, social, reasonable: this is no longer the French language but human language, and this is why those in power had recourse to it in their treatises; . . . henceforth the interests of the people and the will of kings will be founded upon a more solid base; war will no longer be sown in the languages of peace.*" And here is the footnote: "*One of the judges of Charles I saved himself with an equivocation: *Si alii consentiunt, ego non dissentio*. He punctuated thus: *Ego non; dissentio*." Finally, as for the papal bull condemning Michel de Bay (Baïus), Voltaire writes: "There was one particular sentence, however, in which, by the change of a comma, certain opinions of Michel Baïus were either condemned or admitted." Voltaire, *The Age of Louis XIV: To which is Added an Abstract of the Age of Louis XV*, trans. R. Griffith (London: Fielding and Walking, 1880), 359.

10. Theodor Adorno, "Punctuation Marks," in *Notes on Literature*: "[Quotation marks] are to be rejected as an ironic device. For they exempt the writer from the spirit whose claim is inherent in irony, and they violate the very concept of irony by separating it from the matter at hand and presenting a predetermined judgment on the subject. The abundant ironic quotation marks in Marx and Engels are the shadows that totalitarian methods cast in advance upon their writings, whose intention was the opposite" (94).

11. Charles Fourier, *Le Nouveau monde industriel et sociétaire, ou Invention du procédé d'industrie attrayante et naturelle distribuée en series passionnées* (Paris: Bossange Père, 1829), 568.

12. Paul Valéry, *Cahiers* (Paris: Gallimard, 1973), 1:473–74.

13. Alain Badiou, *Logics of Worlds: Being and Event*, 2, trans. Alberto Toscano (London: Verso, 2009), 51. This theory is already announced in the first book (50–54).

14. Which does not amount—far from it—to turning it into a supposed indecision that Badiou believes he can diagnose in a certain deconstructive heritage of Heidegger. In fact, despite his belated homage to Derrida in "Notes, Commentaries, and Digressions," gathered in the appendix to *Logics of Worlds*, there is no doubt that, in Badiou's eyes, Derridean deconstruction is liable to the same diagnostic as is Philippe Lacoue-Labarthe, who is afflicted with "a sort of incapacity to decide that is typical . . . of a certain Heideggerian thought" (Alain Badiou, *Five Lessons on Wagner*, trans. Susan Spitzer [London: Verso Books, 2010], 17).

14 / Final Survey

1. Walter Benjamin, *Gesammelte Schriften*, vol. 6, ed. Rolf Tiedemann and Hermann Schweppenhäuser (Frankfurt am Main: Suhrkamp, 1985), 205. [The translation attempts to follow the author's French translation as closely as possible.—Trans.]

2. As I write these lines, it is being debated in U.S. courts whether "A 'Like' on Facebook amounts to freedom of expression" (this is the title of the AFP dispatch

announcing the legal case initiated by the American Civil Liberties Union and Facebook, a dispatch reprinted in *Le Monde*, 9 August 2012). On a different note, I read on mixdiscount.com the following clause in the "general conditions of sale" ("article 5: electronic signature"): "The purchaser's 'click' to place an order constitutes an electronic signature that has the same value between parties as a handwritten signature."

3. Martin Heidegger, "European Nihilism," in *Nietzsche*, vol. 3, ed. David Farrell Krell (New York: Harper Collins, 1991). In "The Word of Nietzsche: 'God Is Dead,'" Heidegger speaks of "thinking in terms of values." In Heidegger, *The Question concerning Technology and Other Essays*, trans. William Lovitt (New York: Garland, 1977), 53–112.

4. Carl Schmitt, *Die Tyrannei der Werte* (Berlin: Duncker & Humblot, 2011), 42. A few pages above this (38), Schmitt cites Heidegger at length ("The Word of Nietzsche: 'God Is Dead'").

5. George Gallup and Saul Forbes Rae, *The Pulse of Democracy: The Public-Opinion Poll and How It Works* (New York: Simon and Schuster, 1940). Loïc Blondiaux (*La Fabrique de l'opinion: Une Histoire sociale des sondages* [Paris: Le Seuil, 1998]) mentions the "editorial innovation" that was the creation, in July 1935, of the column "The Fortune Survey" in *Fortune* magazine, a column that proposed to "take account, four times a year, of the results of a survey undertaken by questionnaire filled out by 3,000 American adults concerning their attitudes towards various current themes" (158). A few months later, in October 1935, George Gallup, who had created his own polling institute (the American Institute of Public Opinion), signed "a publication agreement with about sixty American newspapers" (158). Blondiaux also cites (52–53, 56) various antecedents to the modern poll, such as the inquiry launched by the controller general of finances, Orry, in 1745 (for which the stewards of the realm were to "spread the rumor . . . of an increase of one third on the customs duty" and to "carefully collect what the inhabitants are going to say about it") or Napoleon I indicating in his *Memorial of Saint Helena* that he received "each month reports on the state of public opinion concerning the acts of government." If Gallup is thus no doubt not the first pollster in history, "his figure," Blondiaux writes, "imposes itself to the point where the word *Gallup* very quickly becomes synonymous with polls in nearly all Western nations" (160).

6. Several times, in order to explain didactically the statistical principle of the sample, Gallup compares the process of taking samples to tallying words in stenography or dactylography. "There is nothing startling or magical about sampling" (56), he thus writes: "The stenographer who hurriedly counts a single line of her typing to see how many words she has typed on the page is taking a rough 'sample'" (56). Later, Gallup uses the same example to illustrate the problem of the representativity of the sample: "While some lines may contain only short words like 'and' and 'but,' other lines will consist of words like 'anticonstitutional' or 'paleontological.' In order to obtain a fairly accurate estimate of the total number of words on the page, she must select a line that contains a typical proportion of both short and long words, so that it will be representative of the lines on the entire page. If this is difficult to do by inspection alone, she will probably select several lines" (59). Extending the metaphor, one could thus say that it is as though the opinion poll assumed a *praelectio* that spaces the *scriptio continua* of the sociopolitical text.

7. In this sense, the poll is in fact understood as one of the "inventions which might make democracy work more effectively" (11). Gallup here inscribes himself in the heritage of the theories of James Bryce (author of *The American Commonwealth* in 1888

and of *Modern Democracies* in 1920), whom he cites as the prophet of the "fourth stage of democracy" ("The Fourth Stage of Democracy" is the title of the ninth chapter of *The Pulse of Democracy*). See especially: "In visualizing the future, Bryce made a statement of prophetic import: 'A fourth stage would be reached,' he wrote, 'if the will of the majority of citizens were to become ascertainable at all times'" (125).

8. Gabriel Tarde, *Monadologie et sociologie* (1893; Paris: Synthélabo, 1999), §4. Remarking that "science tends . . . to generalize the notion of society strangely," Tarde thus considers the existence "of animal societies . . . , of cellular societies, and, why not, of atomic societies," which he later characterizes (§6) as peopled by "infinitesimal citizens of mysterious cities." How not to think of Nietzsche, who in a posthumous fragment from 1885 described the "human body" as "an immense gathering of living beings, all dependent and subordinated, but in another sense dominant and acting according to their own will"? (cited and commented on by Barbara Stiegler in her remarkable opuscule *Nietzsche et la biologie* [Paris: Presses Universitaires de France, 2001], 25). It so happens, moreover, that Tarde's reference to Nietzsche's thought is made explicit, as is testified to by this passage from his *Psychologie économique*, vol. 1 (Paris: Félix Alcan, 1902), where it is precisely a question of the *measure of values*: "Every epoch, every civilization, according to Nietzsche, has what he calls '*a table of values*.' . . . We would not take issue with Nietzsche over either the existence or the capital importance of this table of values he speaks of. But it supposes, above all, that there are social *quantities*. For, if a thing is to be reputed *more* or *less* than another, do they not have to have a common measure?—We must therefore accept *social quantities*" (66n2).

9. *Zurückhören* ("to hear in the past" [*entendre dans le passé*], in André Préau's translation) appears just once in *The Principle of Reason*, suggesting a movement that we could qualify as *archeotology*.

Index

VERBAL ARTS :: STUDIES IN POETICS

Lazar Fleishman and Haun Saussy, series editors